WOMANIST SASS and TALK BACK

WOMANIST SASS and TALK BACK

Social (In)Justice, Intersectionality, and Biblical Interpretation

Mitzi J. Smith

CASCADE *Books* · Eugene, Oregon

WOMANIST SASS AND TALK BACK
Social (In)Justice, Intersectionality, and Biblical Interpretation

Cascade Books
An Imprint of Wipf and Stock Publishers
199 W. 8th Ave., Suite 3
Eugene, OR 97401

www.wipfandstock.com

PAPERBACK ISBN: 978-1-4982-8886-6
HARDCOVER ISBN: 978-1-4982-8888-0
EBOOK ISBN: 978-1-4982-8887-3

Cataloging-in-Publication data:

Names: Smith, Mitzi Jane

Title: Womanist sass and talk back : social (in)justice, intersectionality, and biblical interpretation / by Mitzi J. Smith.

Description: Eugene, OR : Cascade, 2018 | Includes bibliographical references.

Identifiers: ISBN 978-1-4982-8886-6 (paperback) | ISBN 978-1-4982-8888-0 (hardcover) | ISBN 978-1-4982-8887-3 (ebook)

Subjects: LCSH: Bible—Hermeneutics. | Bible—Feminist criticism. | Womanist theology.

Classification: LCC BS521.2 S65 2018 (print) | LCC BS521.2 (ebook)

Manufactured in the U.S.A.   01/17/18

We the author and the publisher, are grateful for permission to reprint the following copyrighted material.

©Mitzi J. Smith, "Race, Gender, and the Politics of 'Sass': Reading Mark 7:24–30 Through a Womanist Lens of Intersectionality and Inter(con)textuality," in *Womanist Interpretations of the Bible. Expanding the Discourse,* eds. Gay L. Byron and Vanessa Lovelace (Atlanta: Society of Biblical Literature Press, 2016) 95–112. Used by permission of Society of Biblical Literature Press.

©Mitzi J. Smith, "Slavery, Torture, Systemic Oppression, and Kingdom Rhetoric: An African American Reading of Matthew 25:1–13," in *Insights from African American Interpretation* (Minneapolis: Fortress, 2017) 77–97. Used by permission of Fortress Press.

Contents

CHAPTER ONE

Introduction

Our backs
Tell stories
No books have
The spine to
Carry
—women of color

By Rupi Kaur[1]

Over the years I have become more critically aware of and passionate about the injustices to which the most vulnerable in our societies are subjected on a daily basis. And I have pondered the ways in which I integrate my passions for social justice with my teaching, preaching, and writing. I know that too many of my students and other readers of sacred texts have been taught and encouraged to suffer injustices in silence. In various ways readers are taught to ignore their pain and to stifle their struggles (and those of others) by reading from positions of privilege. Some readers are convinced that it is sacrilegious to question or critique the sacred text, to struggle with it or with characterizations of God in the text. My aim is to prioritize the oppressions and injustices that daily threaten and take the lives of the most vulnerable and to demonstrate other ways of reading that

1. Kaur, *Milk and Honey*, 171.

1

do not trick or force readers to become complicit in their own oppressions and oppression of others.

Biblical interpretation or scholarship is primarily concerned with the world behind the text (the historical) and/or the world the text constructs (the literary) and only marginally addresses the world in front of the text or contemporary (con)texts. But the impact of our contemporary context, like air in the room, is inescapable; it is the elephant in the room and sometimes the elephant is the room. To expect communities most impacted by social injustice to ignore their oppressions in the process of interpretation places a greater and often unbearable burden on them as readers of sacred texts. When members of minoritized oppressed communities are asked and expected to treat social (in)justice issues that impact their daily lives as a postscript to authentic biblical interpretation, their voices are silenced and marginalized and are often unwittingly taught to accept the imposed silence as a sacred obligation and sacrifice that God requires.

In this book, I read sacred texts from and with my locatedness and my embodiment as an African American female biblical scholar. I read from my position and perspective in front of the text, as a person of color who wishes to acknowledge and address the oppression and the suffering of communities of color. Some significant issues of social injustice that impact poor communities of color and particularly African American women, children, and men are placed in dialogue with sacred (con)texts, creating a strategic inter(con)textuality between ancient and living and contemporary testimonies or stories. Injustices in our world summon us to read the sacred (con)texts in ways that reflect and embody the Goddess-God that loves justice and summons us to do justice. God empathizes with and responds to the predicament of the oppressed. God is a living God who continues to inspire and interact with readers to form new, free, life-giving testimonies.

The readings in this book are both inter(con)textual and intersectional. My reading perspective is a womanist intersectional approach that privileges or prioritizes the experiences, voices, traditions, and artifacts of African American women (and their communities) as sources of knowledge production, critical reflection, and ethical conduct. Womanism as a political movement seeks to dismantle oppression in all of its forms and is especially concerned with the ways that bias and oppression based on race, gender, class, and/or sexuality intersect and mutually impact the lives of African American women and other people of color. Womanism as a political movement begins with a commitment to and consciousness of black women's need for self-love, self-care, and liberation from physical, mental, and spiritual bondage and systemic social injustice or oppression. Self-love and self-care are prerequisites for neighbor and other-directed love and care. Black feminist bell hooks states that self-care for black women is a political act of resistance.[2] Womanism as a political movement seeks, promotes, and embodies the well-being of black women and men, the wholeness of entire communities of color, and a global neighbor-love. I wrote this book as an act of self-care, of political resistance to contemporary and ancient (con) texts that threaten, oppose, or are antithetical to the self-care and wholeness of the oppressed. Biblical interpretation is a political act and can be an act of social justice or injustice. I write as an act of womanist resistance, an act of sass and talk-back to (con)texts that disturbingly re-inscribe structures of oppression and are oppressive, that invite us to be complicit in oppression, that primarily depict God as a violent male, that subordinate the other, and that embody and sacralize (the secular is elevated to the level of the sacred) androcentrism, patriarchalism, and misogyny.

Alice Walker, in her book *In Search of Our Mothers' Gardens*, defines a womanist as a woman of color who behaves and talks audaciously and who is serious, in charge.[3] Womanists boldly use our agency to interpret sacred texts for ourselves and in ways that free us and our communities from constructions of God that further oppress us and that condone violence on the basis of gender, race, class, sexuality, and othering. I read sacred texts in ways that are relevant to folks who stand daily with their backs against the wall. Relevant and contextual critical biblical interpretation attempts to expose and condemn oppression and violence in sacred (con)texts. Like the Scriptures, black, brown, and yellow bodies and their communities are sacred (con)texts. When we turn a blind eye to biases and violence in our sacred (con)texts, the likelihood is great that we will learn to internalize the oppression in (con)texts and read as oppressed people, rather than as a people who value and seek freedom for ourselves and for others. We are traumatized and we will traumatize others.

Writing this book was personally therapeutic. It became a space where I could release and deal with some of my own posttraumatic stress from watching too many videos of black men, women, and children killed as a result of encounters with police officers or who were violently yanked out of a classroom chair or flung across the room like a bag of trash. The

2. hooks, *Sisters of the Yam,* 7.
3. Walker, *In Our Mothers' Gardens,* ix.

3

contemporary justice issues this womanist project addresses include the water shut offs in Detroit (and the Flint water crises), unjust systems/structures, police brutality and profiling in poor communities of color, oppressive pedagogy, and sexual violence. The social (in)justice issues addressed in this book are those that impact the communities where I live and teach in the Detroit metropolitan area and that impact women and communities of colors in cities like Ferguson, Missouri; Baltimore, Maryland; Minnesota; Cleveland, Ohio, and places in between and beyond.

Although therapy encourages us toward wholeness, it is never easy; it in fact can be quite painful to confront, honestly, what ails or haunts us. Writing this book was more difficult than I anticipated both because of the subject matter and because of an added responsibility that I assumed. I chose to become a foster parent with the intention to adopt; it did not work out for the child and me. I do not regret the time we spent as parent and child. And I have not yet given up on her or on providing a permanent home for a child or teenager. Trauma caused by violence and oppression is difficult and sometimes impossible to overcome. The traumatized child often resists attachment to persons that attempt to love her and to help her become free from violence that haunts and from suppressed hauntings. We traumatize ourselves and our children when we allow them to believe that the violence they experience is God's will or that God sanctions violence so that we might find God. Critical biblical interpretation can function (a) as a means of conscientization about oppression embedded in sacred texts and in society and that gets falsely attributed to God; (b) to demonstrate connections between contemporary ideologies that undergird social injustice and oppressive ideologies in sacred (con)texts and interpretations of those (con)texts; and (c) as a source of hope and courage, reminding us that God is on the side of the oppressed and justice.

Many readers are uncomfortable with moral ambiguity in sacred narratives, seeking to align their own lives with the perceived and presumed clear or unambiguous ethical commands and characterizations of God and God's heroes and heroines in sacred texts. Interests, ideologies, and movements attributed to the divine are often sacralized and androcentric (male centered) concerns and prescriptives masquerade as divine mandates. Sacred narratives written and interpreted from the perspective of the winners have the power to further oppress and police the marginalized, minoritized and/or subordinated or the losers, and to persuade the latter to think and behave in ways that do not serve the interests of justice, equity, peace, and love in the earth.

Chapters 2 and 3 of this book construct inter(con)textuality between the injustices that contemporary women of color are experiencing and the stories of two female characters in the biblical text. In Chapter 2, "Water Is a Human Right, but It Ain't Free," I read the encounter between Jesus and the Samaritan woman at the well from the perspective of the Detroit water shut offs that began in 2014 and continue to this day. Most of the poor in the city of Detroit are African American mothers and their children who simply cannot afford to pay the increasing cost of water. But many stereotype Detroit residents as lazy Jezebels who do not want to pay their bills. Similarly readers have stereotyped the Samaritan woman as a Jezebel that Jesus saves. God knows the stories of the Detroiters impacted by the water shut offs like he knows the Samaritan woman's story, and he condemns neither one of them. In fact, Jesus's offer of living water is pivotal to the narrative and can be compared to the United Nation's declaration that water is a human right. Jesus's offer is subversive to empire. In Chapter 3, "Race, Gender and the Politics of 'Sass,'" I read the story of the Syrophoenician woman in Mark's Gospel through the interpretative lens of the Sandra Bland story. Bland was the African American woman whose encounter with a police officer over an alleged failure to signal before she switched lanes ended with her death in a Texas jail cell. For both women, sass and talk-back functioned as a language of resistance.

In Chapter 4, "Epistemologies, Pedagogy, and the Subordinated Other," I argue that the stories of the Ethiopian Eunuch and the Alexandrian Jewish man Apollos in the Acts of the Apostles are parallel characters. I read the two narratives inter(con)textually with the liberative pedagogies of African American women of color, together with my own scholarly personal narrative. Chapter 5, "Slavery, Torture, Systemic Oppression and Kingdom Rhetoric" offers an African American reading of Matthew 25:1–13. I argue that the parable of the ten virgins is part of a trilogy of slave parables that reinscribe oppressive structures. Reading with slave testimony and postcolonial and social political theory, I problematize master-slave ideology and kingdom of heaven rhetoric as appropriate metaphors for God and God's power and presence.

In Chapters 6 and 7 biblical texts are read inter(con)textually with the contemporary issue of police brutality and police sexual misconduct. In Chapter 6, "Moral Authority, Insignificant Young Bodies and Sacralized

Violence," I read 2 Kings 2:23–25 through the lens of racial profiling and police brutality against young African American males. I draw upon group-position and power-threat theories to understand the racial divide when it comes to perspectives and experiences of policing and brutality. With Chapter 7, "A Womanist Reading of Susanna: Patriarchal Authority, Sexual Violence, and Profiling Women of Color," I move beyond the Protestant canon to read the apocryphal text of Susanna inter(con)textually with the contemporary issue of sexual harassment and violence that women of color experience from police officers. When misogynistic men control and constitute the justice system, vulnerable women are not safe, not even women of relative privilege. Often the smallest act of resistance to oppression can have far-reaching consequences. Sometimes multidimensional forms of oppression that a woman faces force her to triage by responding to the most imminent threat that from her perspective carries the grimmest consequences for her quality of life.

CHAPTER TWO

Water is a Human Right, but It *Ain't* Free

A Womanist Reading of John 4:1–42

Context always matters. In the summer of 2014, the City of Detroit began shutting off water to thousands of residential customers unable to pay their water bills, while service to businesses with past due accounts in the tens and hundreds of thousands of dollars remained uninterrupted.[1] In 2017 too many poor residents in the City of Detroit still live without running water.[2] The City of Detroit is not the only city to shut off water to residents; other cities in Michigan like Hamtramck, as well as the cities of Baltimore and St. Louis have done the same.[3] The nearby city of Flint, Michigan, began shutting off water to 8,000 customers in the spring of 2017 for nonpayment of water bills; Flint residents have been exposed to tainted water that they can neither use nor drink since 2014. Flint residents are still visiting water stations and toting water, corrosive infrastructures that make water unsafe to drink have not been repaired, and residents are wondering where all the politicians have gone—the ones that used their city as a political platform during the presidential primaries.

When Detroit residents were deprived of access to water, local activists, churches, and nonprofit organizations rallied to purchase water and

1. Chapman, "Detroit Shuts Off Water."

2. Filson, "After Years of Crisis Detroit Residents are Demanding Affordable Water Legislation."

3. Wisely, "Detroit Not Alone in Shutting Off Water for Unpaid Bills."

other supplies for drinking, hygiene, sanitation, and cooking. Persons around the USA and beyond, including neighboring Canada, assisted in the humanitarian crises.[4] One of my students that works with a local non-profit created specifically to respond to the water-shut-off crises asked me to write something about it on my blog, and I did. Other colleagues and I also delivered water and donated funds to buy water. A few businesses opened their doors for people to use their facilities for bathing. A human being can survive for weeks without food but for only a few days without water. As crucial and as much as our individual responses matter to people denied access to water because they cannot keep up with the rising costs,[5] our efforts are like trying to put expired adhesive bandages on gaping, fatal wounds.

It is in this context that I read the encounter between the Samaritan woman and Jesus at the well (John 4:1–42) inter(con)textually and from the perspective of an African American womanist biblical scholar and ordained minister living in the Detroit metropolitan area and witnessing the tragedy of the Detroit water crises. My womanist interpretative framework focuses on the intersectionality of race, gender, sexuality, class, and neocolonialism. A womanist lens prioritizes and values the voices and experiences of black women and communities of color. In this reading of Jesus' interaction with the Samaritan woman, I place the story in dialogue with the multidimensional oppression that black women experience, complemented by a necessary postcolonial critique. Historically, (neo)colonialism, capitalism, and religious ideologies have collaborated to create an incubator and foundation for structures that allow for the discrimination of poor minoritized peoples, especially poor black women.

Too many readers have treated Jesus' revelation about the Samaritan woman's domestic history and current living situation as the most significant aspect of the narrative, particularly since the woman responds by identifying Jesus as a prophet. But I argue that a more remarkable revelation occurs earlier in the narrative when Jesus claims to possess "living water," which the Samaritan woman can possess merely by asking for it. I further argue that Jesus's assertion that he possesses free living water that he can gift to the Samaritan woman, whose nearest water source is a well in a rural

4. Helms, "Canadians Deliver Water to Protest Detroit Shutoffs."

5. In November, a man reported on a Facebook post that his water bill tripled within a few months. He went from paying $100 every three months for water to paying $100 every month in a very short time. Stories like this abound.

community, is a subversive claim against the Roman Empire, known for its great aqueducts through which flowed living water. The dialogue between Jesus and the Samaritan woman signifies a shared cultural recognition of water as a human right, regardless of one's race/ethnicity, class, or gender.

A WOMANIST LENS: WATER IS A HUMAN RIGHT, BUT IT *AIN'T* FREE!

According to the 2010 US Census data, 82.7 percent of the City of Detroit is Black non-Hispanic; 6.8 percent is Hispanic, and 10.6 percent is White.[6] Between the 2000 and 2010 Census data, the City of Detroit experienced a dramatic 25 percent decline in population.[7] Twenty-six percent of the population is under eighteen years of age; 52.7 percent of the population is female. The average number of occupants in a house is 2.7 percent with a median household income of $26,955. That figure is much lower than the median household income for the state of Michigan, which is $48,471. Thirty-eight percent of persons living in the City of Detroit are below the poverty level. We do not know how many languish at cents above the superficial poverty level. That rate is more than double the percentage of 16.3 percent living below the poverty level in the state of Michigan. Most likely, the majority of Detroiters impacted by the water shut offs are poor, black, and female with children.

In March 2013, Michigan Governor Rick Snyder appointed an Emergency Manager (EM) for the City of Detroit, and in July 2013 Detroit became the largest US city to file for bankruptcy. When an EM is appointed, elected city officials are forced to yield significant powers to the EM. The EM began his job in Detroit with sweeping powers, thanks to a revised state law governing EMs, which was enacted the same week the Detroit EM began his work in the city. Many citizens regarded the seizure of power by the state as "unconstitutional" and "undemocratic."[8] The institution of the revised laws regarding state takeover of cities like Detroit and the appointment of an EM

6. US Census Bureau, State and County QuickFacts, Detroit (city of), Michigan.

7. Chicago experienced a 7 percent decline in the same period; and Cleveland, Ohio, a 17 percent decline. "2010 Census Data for City of Detroit Neighborhoods, April 5, 2011."

8. Davey, "Bankruptcy Lawyer is Named to Manage an Ailing Detroit." In November 2014, the EM announced that his job was almost complete; the bankruptcy plan for the city was approved.

with sweeping powers has also been called "domestic neocolonialism."[9] The latest impact of this "domestic neocolonialism" under the EM has been the shut-off of water to thousands of Detroit residents—a move that disproportionately impacts the most vulnerable and poor in the city.

In April 2014 the Detroit Water and Sewerage Department (DWSD) began shutting off water to thousands of Detroiters whose water rates had more than doubled over the past ten years. DWSD shut off water to 7,000 separate residential customers between April and June of that year. That same June the city approved an 8.7 percent increase in water rates.[10] And the poorest citizens were not exempt. At one point, the courts granted a short moratorium before DWSD resumed shutting off water to residents. Any resident owing $150 or more (by some accounts less than $150) or who was sixty days in arrears were slated to have the water shut off.[11] Activists, churches, nonprofits, and individual citizens scrambled to purchase bottled water, donate, and set up stations to receive water for their neighbors. Payment plans were made available to some residents, but what happens when people cannot make the payments and/or sign up for plans they know they cannot afford?[12]

In October 2014 Special Rapporteurs (independent investigators) from the United Nations (UN) visited Detroit to listen to the residents and to hear their stories in their own words. Activists had taken the struggle to the UN steps and to national media outlets. Prior to the arrival of the Special Rapporteurs, the UN issued a news release in which it referred to the water shutoffs in Detroit as a violation of human rights:

> Disconnection of water services because of failure to pay due to lack of means constitutes a violation of the human right to water and other international human rights. . . . Because of a high poverty rate and a high unemployment rate, relatively expensive water bills in Detroit are unaffordable for a significant portion of the population.[13]

In a historic move, on July 28, 2010 (almost four years prior to the Detroit shut offs) the UN General Assembly "recognized" water and sanitation

---

9. Rice, "The Neocolonial City."

10. Guillen, "Detroit City Council Approves 8.7 percent Water Rate Increase."

11. Pyke, "Detroit Shuts off Water to Thousands of Broke Residents."

12. *Los Angeles Times*, "Detroit Water Shut-offs for Overdue Bills Begin Once Again."

13. Trainor, "Detroit Water Crisis—a Prelude to the Privatization of Water," 1.

as a human right.[14] Bolivia's Ambassador to the UN, Pablo Solon, spoke to the UN on that day. In his speech Ambassador Solon orally amended the UN resolution to read "recognized" instead of "declared" as an acknowledgement of the pre-existing understanding of water as a human right. Access to water did not become a human right with the UN Declaration; it was already presumed to be a human right. The UN Declaration has the impact of fully recognizing water and sanitation as an independent right rather than as only an element or component "of other rights such as 'the right to an adequate standard of living'" or the "right to life."[15] Ambassador Solon reminded the Assembly that individuals can survive for weeks without food but only a few days without water; that about 65 percent of our bodies, including our blood and brains, is water; *inter alia*, more deaths result from illnesses caused by lack of drinking water and sanitation than by war; and that globally about one in eight people still lack potable water.[16] With US cities like Detroit shutting off water to the poorest residents that number will increase in developed countries, if this practice continues. The "second operative paragraph" of the resolution "calls upon States and international organizations to provide financial resources; capacity-building and technology transfer through international assistance and cooperation, in particular to developing countries, in order to scale up efforts to provide safe, clean, accessible and affordable drinking water and sanitation for all."[17] For individuals who do not make a living wage, "affordable drinking water" will have to be free drinking water. "It is necessary," Ambassador Solon argues, "to call on states to promote and protect the human right to drinking water and sanitation."[18]

It is in light of the global recognition that water is a human right and the ongoing water crises in Detroit and other cities, where many of my students and/or my neighbors live, that I shall read the encounter between Jesus and the Samaritan woman at the well. I read with a womanist lens that values and prioritizes black women's experiences and within an interpretative framework that privileges justice and wholeness for the larger black

---

14. The resolution passed with a unanimous vote (no "no" votes) but with 41 countries abstaining.

15. Solon, "UN Declares Water as Human Right."

16. Ibid., 1.

17. Ibid., 2.

18. Ibid., 3.

community as well as for the global community. Womanism promotes and strives for the health and wholeness of the entire community.[19]

"GIVE ME WATER!" MUTUALITY AND HOSPITALITY

When Jesus stops and rests by the well in Sychar, instead of going into the city with his disciples to purchase food, his actions signify the priority and significance of water for his own survival and for human survival generally. Jesus stops at noon when he is tired and likely parched. He stops at noon because at noon he is thirsty. The Samaritan woman arrives at noon because it is at noon that she needs water. At noon, when the sun is quite hot, may have been an unusual time of day to draw water, as some commentators assert, but people do what they have to do and when they have to do it. Maybe noon on this day was the day a single mother could leave home to get water to meet the needs of her household. Or perhaps, when the woman meets Jesus, it is during her second or third trip to the well, at noon. Or Jesus may have run into the woman at the well during her last visit to the well for the day, or maybe her first of many. Maybe her visit to the well in the heat of the day was not what a more privileged person would do, but it may have been routine for her—the beginning, the middle, or the end of her routine depending on how many times she needs to draw water for drinking, bathing, food preparation, and sanitation. According to the United Nations, in developing countries, in excess of 200 million hours of women's time is consumed daily by collecting and transporting water for domestic purposes.[20] We draw water when we need it. Human need does not always coincide with time of day, access to money, and opportunity.

The socio-historical context of the encounter between the Samaritan woman and Jesus at the well is not, as many commentators suggest, a betrothal scene void of a betrothal.[21] Andrew Arterbury argues persuasively for a socio-historical framework of hospitality rather than the betrothal scene context as put forth by Robert Alter in 1981.[22] Arterbury argues that

19. See, St. Clair, "Womanist Biblical Interpretation," 54–62. St. Clair asserts that womanist biblical hermeneutics is a hermeneutics of wholeness; one that does is not complicit in the oppression of black women or of anyone else.

20. United Nations, "The Human Right to Water and Sanitation."

21. For example, O'Day, Gospel of John, 565.

22. Alter, The Art of Biblical Narrative; also Alter, "Biblical Type Scenes and the Uses of Convention," 355–68.

what Alter described, and others have followed, was really hospitality. The end result of hospitality has often been the giving of a gift to the guest or stranger, and sometimes that gift was a father's daughter as a bride,[23] but not all hospitality relationships ended in a betrothal.[24] When Jesus instructs the Samaritan woman to call her husband, he is not initiating a betrothal, but his "instructions follow the logical progression of events that generally take place when a stranger seeks hospitality. Namely, the Samaritan woman is expected to direct the stranger to a hospitable home or to initiate the process whereby the head of her household will extend an offer of hospitality."[25] However, of course, Jesus has taken the initiative and not the woman, and this may be because of long-term hostilities that existed between the two ethnic groups that they represent. In the second century BCE, the Jewish King John Hyrcanus invaded the Samaritan city of Shechem and destroyed the Samaritan temple. Samaritans rejected a Jerusalem-centered religion.[26] "The more homogeneous Judeans looked upon their northern kin as stained by the blood and customs of their captors."[27] By 107 BCE, Hyrcanus sent most of the people back to the city of Samaria but a residual community remained in Sychar and Neopolis around the base of Gerizim.[28] Such was the state when Jesus met the woman at the well. Within a generation of the encounter between Jesus and the Samaritan woman at the well, Samaritans fleeing Roman oppression gathered at Mt. Gerizim holding the Romans at bay for a month when water ran out and they either died of thirst or were slaughtered by the Roman soldiers.[29]

As Adele Reinhartz asserts, according to the narrative, by asking the woman for water, Jesus crossed ethnic and social boundaries when he spoke to her.[30] I propose that when Jesus asks the woman about her husband,

23. Hospitality has sometimes resulted in the taking and ravishing of a virgin daughter and a concubine as in Judges 19.

24. Arterbury, "Breaking the Betrothal Bonds," 74, 77. Arterbury posits that "in many ancient narratives, the act of betrothal essentially functioned as the pivotal act of a host giving a gift to a guest. When a host gave his daughter as a gift to the guest, it created an intimate and unending relationship. It created a permanent kinship bond or alliance between the two families."

25. Arterbury, "Breaking the Betrothal Bonds," 77.

26. Williamson and Kartveit, "Samaritans," 834–35.

27. Anderson, "Mount Gerizim," 218.

28. Ibid., 219.

29. Ibid.

30. Reinhartz, "Gospel of John," 572.

the narrator, in a roundabout way, constructs a parallel between the Samaritan woman's story and the encounter between Elijah and the widow of Zarephath (1 Kgs 17:10–11). As Gail O'Day notes, "in both stories a man interrupts a woman engaged in household work to request a gesture of hospitality" thus furthering the continuity between Jesus and the prophetic tradition.[31] Also for both stories, the context is journey and the lack of/need for water: the demand for water from the prophet initiates the encounter and the encounter takes places at a boundary marker (the city gate for Elijah and Jacob's well for Jesus). Neither Elijah nor Jesus is seeking a wife for himself or for anybody else, and both women are living with or taking care of a male who is not her husband.

Just as Elijah demands water from the widow of Zarephath (1 Kgs 17:10c), Jesus does not ask for water, but he demands it: "Give me [some water] to drink" (*Dos moi pein*) (4:7). *Dos* is aorist imperative; the imperative mood is the grammatical mood of demand or command. Jesus commands that the Samaritan woman gives him water based on a basic human need within a culture of expected hospitality among human beings, particularly toward the stranger and/or other vulnerable persons in their midst (e.g., Deut 17:18). It is the language of hospitality. Jesus' demand signifies a shared cultural understanding of hospitality; this hospitality transcends ethnic, religious, class, and gender boundaries. The narrative alerts the reader that Jesus' disciples went into the city to buy food and thus chose not to chance acquiring food and water (hospitality) among the rural people in Sychar with whom they have not always been on good terms. So that we are left with a single weary male traveler rather than a group of men, which makes Jesus' request for hospitality more difficult to ignore and to deny—one human being calling upon another human being to meet a human need, irrespective of gender, ethnicity/race, or class.

We can conceive of the disciples collectively as representing or symbolic of a system or a structure of bias. Structures and systems based in discriminatory difference are more difficult to permeate, to transcend and/or dismantle, as manifested by the collective, homogenous response of the disciples when they see Jesus interacting with the Samaritan woman (4:27–33). It appears that the disciples did not expect anyone in Sychar to provide free hospitality to Jesus, seemingly on the grounds of ethnic and religious difference. They assumed no one would transcend the multi-millennial old boundaries of mutual hostility and discrimination. Sychar,

31. O'Day, *Gospel of John*, 565.

ancient Shechem, consisted of an ethnically/racially homogenous population of Samaritans who were historically a mixed brood (2 Kgs 17).

But Jesus' story of needing water, his story, transcends their inimical history, just as human need transcends ethnicity/race, gender, and class. The Samaritan woman responds to Jesus' demand with a question: "How is it that you, a Jew, ask a drink of me, a woman of Samaria?" (4:9, NRSV). The Samaritan woman understands Jesus' use of the language of demand as a request for hospitality, from one racial/ethnic person to another. The focus of her question is not on his maleness, but on his racial-ethnic affiliation, on his Jewishness in relation to the request. The difference she raises is not one of gender or of class, but of race/ethnicity. The narrator informs the readers of the discrimination of the Jews toward the Samaritans: "(Jews do not share things in common [Greek: *sugchraomai*][32] with Samaritans.)" (4:9b, NRSV). Verse 11 implies that the thing that Jews don't share with Samaritans is drinking vessels. The narrator informs his audience of a subtext of discrimination on the grounds of what is pure and impure, an ancient invisible structure that is often manifest at the crossroads of human need and the allocation and/or reception of resources. It is a subtext that has and could paralyze one in the face of human need and the necessary human response of hospitality. The shared experiences of Jews and Samaritans include not only the expectation of hospitality toward the stranger within their gates, but of justified discrimination. Samaritanism is a form of Judaism (4:12, 20; Gen 33:18–20; 2 Kgs 17). As Teresa Okure asserts, the "shared experiences of prejudice, racism, and sexism flowing from the social norms of their societies" surfaced.[33]

It is not clear how the Samaritan woman knows that Jesus is a Jew; maybe we are to presume he identified himself as a Jew, perhaps his cloak or other clothing betray his ethnicity. At John 8:48 Jesus is accused by "the Jews" of being a Samaritan and having a demon; he categorically denies having a demon, but does not address the former accusation. A Samaritan might be less likely to make the same mistake. After the Samaritan woman raises the obvious question of ethnic difference, Jesus reveals his divine connection and his ability to give free living water to her (4:10). And the woman responds in the similar language of hospitality in the imperative

---

32. For a discussion of the meaning of this Greek word as "to use something together with another person" in John see Daube, "Jesus and the Samaritan Woman: The Meaning of συγχραομαι."

33. Okure, "Jesus and the Samaritan Woman (JN 4:1–42) in Africa," 416.

mood: "Give me this water" (*dos moi touto to hydōr*) (4:11). The water Jesus offers the Samaritan woman is free, just as the hospitality Jesus expects from her is free. In exchange for a one-time act of hospitality, Jesus is offering the woman a free life-time supply of water, of life-giving and life-sustaining water. The woman would love it if she no longer had to make several trips a day to the well to draw water. Although Jesus may have in mind spiritual water, spiritual water cannot substitute for access to physical water. Yung Suk Kim argues that, "in the socio-religious context of discrimination, the metaphor of spiritual water can be understood as collapsing the hostile barriers between Jews and Gentile in that the water symbolizes abundant life and equality for all."[34] However, I argue that Jesus' offer of living water to the Samaritan woman with whom he shares the experience of colonization under the Roman Empire signifies a point of convergence and of correspondence for colonized peoples who can have access to water, living water, independent of their colonizers. Thus, living water functions as a unifying metaphor, transcending its symbolism—a metaphor of interdependence between two colonized peoples and independence from total dependence on the Roman Empire as colonizer. According to Kim the abundant life for all offered by the living water "includes personal, communal, and global aspects of life: as seen in the expansion from the Samaritan woman, to her village, and to the world."[35] But I would further differ and argue that within this global framework living water is more than a spiritual reality, but becomes a human and material right as well based on its significance for human life. Who can live an abundant life without the necessities of life? John's Jesus does not spiritualize or trivialize the resources, such as water and nourishment that people need for daily sustenance (2:1–11). If John's Jesus will adjust his schedule to provide wine from water for a wedding feast, he surely must be concerned that humans have access to physical water. Indeed, he stopped at Sychar because of his need to quench his physical thirst for water.

34. Kim, *Truth, Testimony, and Transformation*, 39.
35. Ibid.

THE POLITICS OF WATER: LIVING WATER, CLASSISM, AND A POSTCOLONIAL OPTIC

The planned water shutoffs to tens of thousands of Detroiters may be a prelude to the privatization of water.[36] When natural resources are harnessed and commodified for the purpose of yielding high revenues, human need is not a priority. The control and allocation of water is political and always privileges the wealthiest consumers. Inga Winkler, a Legal Advisor to the UN Special Rapporteur on the Human Right to Safe Drinking Water and Sanitation, argues that, "addressing the crisis in the lack of access of water requires, of course, water resources. . . Yet above all, it requires the political will to use these resources in a way to prioritise [sic] basic human needs"; it is both a management and a political issue.[37] Winkler further argues that although sufficient water exists "to satisfy the basic household requirement of all people, the entire societal demand for water often exceeds availability; thus, competing interests require that we set priorities for allocating water for the purpose of meeting basic human needs."[38] Privatization of water is a form of neocolonialism wherein interest in profits trumps sustainable solutions and human need. When private companies privilege profits and stock/stakeholder approval, there is little, if any concern, for the public good and customer satisfaction. Profits are aggressively pursued at the expense of water quality and customer care. And rather than protect existing supplies, enhance conservation efforts, help vulnerable populations, curtail pollution and raise public consciousness, increasingly government officials are resorting to privatization. Since water is not a luxury item that people can live without, customers are pressured to either pay the higher prices resulting from privatization or go without access to water and sanitation. In fact, the World Bank (WB) has made it a requirement for loaning money to countries that they privatize their water.[39]

36. Citizen, "Top Ten Reasons to Oppose Water Privatization."

37. Winkler, *The Human Right to Water,* 7.

38. Ibid.

39. Citizen, "Top Ten Reasons to Oppose Water Privatization." According to Barlow and Clarke ("Water Privatization"), the WB has been pushing the commodification of water for some time leaving millions of people without water. In 2004 ten major corporations were delivering water and wastewater services to over 300 million customers in 100 countries, and they continue to grow exponentially. It was estimated that by 2014 the top three providers would control 70 percent of the market in Europe and North America. The WB has been the principal financier of privatized water, and the WB has required the privatization of water by countries seeking loans for water. Privatization has resulted

In the story of the interaction between the Samaritan woman and Jesus, as well as in other biblical (con)texts, access to water is political. Because water is necessary for life, people form alliances in order to obtain greater access to water. In prophetic oracles, Israel and/or Judah are accused of forsaking God, the source and provider of living water in order to have what they perceive as greater access to the precious resource. In a vision of Deutero-Zech regarding the eschatological day of the Lord, a late fifth-century BCE prophecy regarding the return of the colonized exiles to Jerusalem to rebuild the city and temple, the exiles are promised a future in which the city will have unrestrained access to living water: Zech 14:8LXX states that, "living waters (*hydōr zōn*) will flow out of Jerusalem." The Greek construction in the LXX is the same as at John 4:10 (*hydōr zōn*). It is a promise of independence in the midst of their colonialization; they will not need to depend on their colonizers for the most valuable and needful substance for all life. At Jer 2:13LXX, YHWH is referred to as a "well of living water" in an oracle to the house of Israel because they committed two evils (1) forsook YHWH as the fountain of living water, giving their allegiance to other gods and nations; and (2) dug cisterns for themselves that hold no water. Similarly, at Jer 17:13LXX, Judah forsook the "fountain or well of life, YHWH." In John 7:38 the Greek construction is the same as at John 4:10 (*hydatos zōntos*) with the use of the participle, except here it is genitive: "*out of the believer's belly shall flow rivers of living water*" because he trusts in God (the thirsty one who comes to Jesus shall drink). Thus, living water is free flowing water from a natural source like a fountain versus stagnant water that might be drawn from a cistern (water tank) or well water. Jesus' offer to give the Samaritan woman living water just for the asking, free of charge, is a subversive anti-colonial gesture. What Jesus offers transcends water sources attributed to humans, including, but not limited to, Jacob's well (4:12–15). Both Jesus and the Samaritan woman belong to peoples colonized under the Roman Empire. While religious differences divide them, their colonial oppression unites them and can be seen as the medium for building or mending their ethnic/racial-theological differences.

Roman urban centers, like Greek cities, relied on a continuous flow of water rather than expecting water on demand as in our society. The result may have been a lot of wasted water, but the constant flow of water

---

in higher prices, lack of transparency, corruption, shutoffs for customers unable to pay, diminished water quality, and large profits. Countries like Senegal and South Africa have turned off water to tens of millions of people, many of whom are forced to use untreated water.

constituted the only option, since aqueducts could not be switched on and off.[40] Rome was the first vast city characterized by its management of drinking water. The Romans relied upon the ideas of many of their foreign predecessors, but they were famous for their aqueducts that carried water via natural gravity, nonstop, to Roman cities. The first Roman aqueduct, the Appia, was constructed in 312 BCE and ten others were added within five centuries. The aqueducts ensured a steady, continuous flow of water to public baths and lavish fountains, and for private homes that could afford to pay taxes on the spigot. The tax, the *vectigal,* was based on the size of the spigot. The *vectigal* helped to pay for the maintenance of the water system; water itself was free, but customers of piped water paid for the delivery of the water into their homes. "To the average Roman resident . . . water in the city was available by right, as free for the taking as water from the Tiber River."[41] Archaeological evidence from the ruins of the Roman city of Pompeii dated around 79 CE shows that piped water was a luxury and access to piped water was potentially a status symbol of wealth and influence.[42] Still the urban population had access to public water supply through huge, elaborately decorated water basins. People living in rural areas, like the Samaritan woman, had access to water via cisterns and wells. *Lacus,* or public water basins, were placed in Roman cities for the benefit of the public who would gather, as at a well, and draw water freely. But the amount of water a person could draw from the *lacus* was limited by the effort and time it took to carry the water from the *lacus* to one's home. The number of *lacus* increased exponentially under Emperor Augustus from ninety-one to about 600. Augustus made an indelible political statement, increasing

40. Fagan, *Elixir,* 184. The Romans excelled in channeling water through rough terrain and across broad plains, which often surrounded their cities. Most the water from Roman aqueducts, about seventeen percent, was consumed for public baths. It was the emperor's responsibility to provide water, but sometimes the wealthy paid for and constructed their own aqueducts. In 19 BCE Marcus Vispanius Agrippa, a prominent statesman, constructed the Aqua Virgo for his own private baths, 194.

41. Salzman, *Drinking Water,* 54–56.

42. Jones and Robinson, "Water, Wealth, and Social Status at Pompeii," 695–710. New archaeological evidence from excavations in Pompeii, particularly regarding the House of the Vestals, demonstrate that in the last part of the first century CE piped pressurized water and water features associated with access to pressurized piped water was a sign of luxury and opulence. Prior to the introduction of piped water via aqueducts, water was used moderately. Thus "a private supply of piped water to a household was costly and available only to a certain sector of society. It is within this context that its role as a luxury product arose and that its ostentatious use in the definition and promotion of social status" is viewed, 699.

public access to water through *lacus*. As the first Emperor after the murder of Julius Caesar, the imperial gesture quite possibly served as a reminder to "the common people that they received their water from imperial beneficence in the name of their ruler. . . . The Roman's right to water was acknowledged, ensured, and enhanced as *Aqua Nomine Caesaris*—water in the name of Caesar."[43] Yet Rome's aqueducts could not have been built without the labor of copious numbers of war prisoners and/or slaves. The construction of the aqueducts by Rome's leaders achieved for them a prestige that, "defined political relationships between the rulers and the ruled."[44] When the Roman Empire collapsed, the aqueducts would eventually cease to flow and what remained was traditional sources of water, e.g., wells and cisterns, which did not require an abundance of prisoners and slave labor.[45]

Thus, for Jesus to offer living water to the Samarian woman may very well have been a subversive, anti-colonial, political proposition. We might presume in her testimony to her neighbors, the Samaritan woman told them about Jesus' offer of living water. And maybe the Samaritan people who responded to her testimony and went to meet Jesus had made this political connection and had to see for themselves. Indeed, they proclaim Jesus to be the "savior of the world" (4:42). As Craig Koester argues the title "savior of the world" was subversive to the Roman Emperor, giving sovereignty to Jesus and not to Rome or the Caesar[46]—a sovereignty that YHWH desired to have from ancient Israel, but instead too often they choose to politically align themselves with those who ostensibly controlled the living water.

(NEO)COLONIAL DISCOURSE AND STEREOTYPES: SEXUALLY IMMORAL AND LAZY WOMEN

The Samaritan woman has been, and continues to be, the victim of stereotyping. Many commentators and readers have stereotyped and/or demonized the Samaritan woman based on her marital history and current living arrangement; she is considered sexually immoral and/or hypersexual and therefore summarily condemned. In a patriarchal society, women's activities in the domestic sphere generally serve to characterize or sum up their entire lives. Ernst Haenchen correctly argues that, "how the woman came

43. Salzman, *Drinking Water*, 56–57.

44. Fagan, *Elixir*, 197.

45. Ibid.

46. Koester, "'The Savior of the World' (John 4:42)," 665–80.

to be married five times holds no significance for the story"; the author does not elaborate on her marital history.[47] More significantly, Jesus presciently reveals her life story, a portion of which the narrator shares with the audience; her marital history and present living situation is only a small portion of her life story. As voyeurs peering and reading into the story, what is not stated, and therefore not factual, as if it is truth, readers have often stereotyped the Samaritan woman as sexually immoral. Many have characterized her in ways that she, Jesus, nor the narrator have done. Some say that Jesus reveals her "immoral life;"[48] exposed her current "sinful situation,"[49] her "sexual irregularities . . . [or] evil deeds,"[50] her "scandalous past,"[51] and that she visits the well at noon because of "public shame."[52] Emmanuel McCall writes, "She was a social outcast. The scripture does not say this, but she was probably an attractive woman. She was at least capable of attracting five husbands. . . . She was seen as a 'serial fornicator.' And perhaps, the secret envy of other women."[53] McCall continues by stating the following: "[Jesus] not only revealed her past, described her present, but like a teacher at a marking board, he wiped the surface clean. What Jesus cleans is always sanitized."[54] Even if readers determine the Samaritan woman's current domestic situation to be ostensibly innocuous or harmless, they still ultimately default on the side of characterizing her as a sinner woman whom Jesus saved, as occurred with some students in my Gospels course. Many readers have either explicitly or implicitly stereotyped the woman as guilty of sexual sin and/or as hypersexual.

The creation of stereotypes is a convenient way to withhold resources from people and/or to treat them in discriminatory ways based on negative difference. Homi Bhabha asserts that, "the construction of the colonial subject in discourse, and the exercise of colonial power through discourse, demands an articulation of forms of difference—racial and sexual."[55] In

47. Haenchen, *John 1*, 221. Similarly, Reinhartz ("The Gospel of John") states that Jesus has shown no interest "in her sexual history per se," 573.

48. Beasley-Murray, *John*, 61.

49. Moloney, *John*, 127. See also Higgs, "The Woman at the Well."

50. Tenney, *Gospel of John*, 55.

51. Boyd, *Repenting of Religion*, 54.

52. Mcleod, "Life-Changing Encounters with Jesus."

53. McCall, "Neither Gerizim nor Zion," 587.

54. Ibid., 589.

55. Bhabha, *The Location of Culture*, 96.

order to justify the shutting off of water to people who cannot pay the rising costs of water, delinquent customers are discursively stereotyped as lazy deadbeats who have too many children and do not want to work and/or pay their utility bills. Historically, African American women have been stereotyped as hypersexual and as lazy, from slavery through to the present. In the early 1990s and beyond, black women were stereotyped as hypersexual, lazy Jezebels through the myth of the welfare queen.[56] More recently, poor black women and their families who have been the victims of the City of Detroit's water shut offs have been depicted by some middle and upper-class folks across racial lines, including within the media, explicitly and implicitly as lazy and hypersexual—or as "welfare queens." Under the myth of the welfare queen, all minoritized women are the same; they are not individuals with life stories; they are not deserving of having their basic human needs met because they are characterized as lazy women who cannot control themselves sexually and who thus keep popping out babies they cannot take care of; they are considered to be primarily poor black and Latina women. While most women on welfare are poor white women, poor black women became the face of welfare and dubbed in 1976 by then presidential candidate Ronald Reagan as "welfare queens." "Welfare queens" are black women and women of color who are hypersexualized and lazy and therefore unworthy of public welfare and compassion. Such stereotypes justify the denial of basic rights including the right to water for poor women of color and their families despite their inability to meet the rising cost of utilities. If they owe $150 (and by some accounts less), their water can be shut off and they can be left to suffer and die with little or no protest.

Some readers cannot escape the mythical story about the Samaritan woman, repeating as putative knowledge or truth a gospel of alternative facts about her sexually checkered past and her present situation of "shacking up" with a man who is not her husband, despite the absence of supporting evidence in the narrative. Readers are expected to know who or what she is and yet they must be told repetitively by interpreters that she is immoral, that Jesus saved her. This is how the stereotype functions, according to Homi Bhabha, as ambivalence, a central process of stereotyping.[57] Ambivalence is the nervous repetition of something that is supposed to be known already. The stereotype has to be repeated to be reinforced. The

56. See Hancock, *The Politics of Disgust.*
57. Bhabha, *Location of Culture.*

force of ambivalence gives the colonial stereotype its common acceptance. "Colonial discourse produces the colonized as a social reality which is at once an 'other' and yet entirely knowable and visible."[58] Thus the stereotype of the Samaritan woman by commentators and preachers has functioned by the production ambivalence of discourse—the ambivalence between what was supposedly known from the text that she was a hypersexual, loose woman, guilty of sexual sin and thus needed to be and was saved by Jesus and the anxious repetition of this supposed truth or fact. In the case of the Samaritan woman, commentators have enhanced the representation of otherness of the woman by articulating sexual difference, in addition to the ethnic or racial difference already stated in the text. According to Bhabha one can only displace stereotyped images by "engaging with its *effectivity*,"[59] that which gives it its power; its ability to produce a result.

Bhabha further argues that, "the stereotype is a simplification . . . because it is an arrested, fixated form of representation"; thus, the Negro remains a Negro wherever he goes.[60] The Samaritan woman remains a sexually immoral woman in many pulpits and bible studies, in some commentaries, and in the "beauty and barber shop" conversations of religious folks. Women who do not conform to the religious beliefs and behaviors of the dominant religion and custodians of the myths are automatically presumed sexually impure and immoral. Indeed, Adele Reinhartz suggests that, "it may be more natural to read it [her marital history and status] as a reflection of the stereotype that Samaritan women are impure and immoral."[61] Bhabha states that, "The same stories are told again and again and afresh—both gratifying and terrifying."[62] In colonial discourses, the black person's skin, his race remains "an ineradicable sign of *negative difference*. . . . For the stereotype impedes the circulation or articulation of the signifier of 'race' as anything other than its *fixity* as racism."[63] For poor black women, it is their skin, gender, and class. For the Samaritan woman, her "five husbands" and the one she is now living with is a *fixity*.

In the welfare queen debates, and in the water crises in Detroit, people assumed a familiarity and fore-knowledge of the stories of the women and

58. Ibid., 101.

59. Ibid., 95.

60. Fanon, *Black Skins, White Masks.*

61. Reinhartz, "John 4:7–42 Samaritan Woman," 454.

62. Bhabha, *Location of Culture*, 111.

63. Ibid., 108.

families that were adversely impacted. In Detroit, some people did not have the chance to tell their stories until the independent investigators representing the UN arrived in Detroit and held hearings. Persons like the emergency manager Kevin Orr have said that people just need to pay their bills. The implication is that people have the money and the resources and just don't *want* to pay their bills; that they are lazy or deceitful. Kevin Orr speaks from a place of privilege that privileges the myth and the stereotypes.

HIS-STORY, HER-STORY, AND GOD'S STORY

The myth created by the discursive repetition of the stereotype is constructed by those who have the power to tell the story and a captive audience. Even when direct speech is attributed to the Samaritan woman, it is not necessarily her story. But we can at least allow the story to be disrupted by, or placed in, dialogue with other stories about women where the author may have had another agenda and therefore let some alternative reality escape through the cracks in the androcentric, colonial text. According to our text, the Samaritan woman is divorced and single but in some kind of domestic relationship with a man, not necessarily sexual, who is not her husband. Other androcentric, patriarchal texts allow that she could have been caught in the cycle of a levirate marriage that requires a deceased man's brother(s) to marry his widow and to produce legitimate heirs, as was the case with Ruth the Moabite daughter-in-law of Naomi (Ruth 1:1–22; Deut 25:5–10). Or her previous husbands could simply have divorced her. It is also possible that her five husbands prematurely and mysteriously died, as was the case with Sarah, Raguel's daughter, who had been married to seven husbands, leaving her with the stigma of being cursed (Tobit 3:7–9). Similarly, Mark 12:18–23 reveals another possible social reality. Some Sadducees related to Jesus the story of a woman who married seven husbands who were brothers and each died leaving the woman a childless widow. In any case, as a single woman, presumably without children, since the narrative mentions none, the Samaritan woman who is not described as a noble woman, but who was likely a woman of little means, would have needed someone to provide her with shelter and other necessities of life. The community was supposed to take care of widows and orphans; so, she may very well have been living with a distant male relative or some other male who loved her but was fearful of marrying her, lest he too die. She could have been doing the best she could in a patriarchal society where a poor woman without a husband would need some kind of male protection.

If and when the Detroiters could tell their stories about having their water shut off, they would differ from the neo-colonial metanarratives discursively constructed with stereotypes. Many of the stories will resemble AtPeace Makita's story. A divorced single mother, AtPeace Makita was one of thousands of Detroit residents whose water was shut off. AtPeace owed only $150 when DWSD shut off her water, but it was $150 she did not have.[64] She is an educated, hardworking woman who was not making enough money to meet all of her children's needs and pay the water bill too. AtPeace became an activist when DWSD cut off water to her household and to thousands of her neighbors. She is an intelligent, talented, vocal young woman who volunteers as creative director for a nonprofit organization called the Detroit Water Brigade (DWB), which solicits donations, acts as a resource for information and for bringing together residents who need water with persons and organizations who can help supply water, among other things. She is an honorable veteran of the US military and a mother of five living children. When asked how having her water shut off impacts her and her family or people in general, AtPeace stated that after a matter of days the state can come in and take away your children and any elderly persons in the home; a person can be evicted immediately and their homes declared unfit. AtPeace's story continues as follows, in her own words:

> I was married and had a family and really felt like my foundation was set . . . when life happened my husband and I separated unexpectedly. Here I am single mother with five children . . . life got real. I had to choose between shoes and the water bill . . . caring for my children and the water bill. The hardest thing was I had to face my children and say "we have no water." It is humiliating. You feel guilty and it's because of the pressure that's put on you in society that if you don't pay your bills you are a delinquent or you are nobody. No consideration of life itself and how life happens to everyone.[65]

Another woman who has one daughter, stated that her water was cut off for a bill of $135. Some people, out of their privilege, cannot imagine how someone could be unable to pay a $135 bill. I can; I can remember not having enough money to catch a bus. I can remember when my mother

64. Trainor, "Detroit Water Crisis."
65. Makita, "Detroit Water Crisis."

25

did not have sufficient change to catch a bus to work. A couple of times, my mother stood at the bus stop, praying and empty handed, hoping for a miracle. On one of those occasions the wind blew a bus ticket into her hand and on the other, a dollar landed at her frozen feet. But most often when she didn't have sufficient bus fare, she walked to work, from one end of the city to another in extreme temperatures. By the time I was ten years old, her legs stopped working.

Forty percent of Detroiters may have lost access to water by the end of the summer of 2014. Yet, major sports facilities in Detroit owed thousands without having their water service interrupted: Palmer Park Golf Club owed $200,000; Joe Louis Red Wings Arena, $80,000; and Ford Field owed $55,000. As the *Michigan Citizen* reported we are witnessing a neo-apartheid.[66]

Many poor people juggle bills from one month to the next, triaging or prioritizing— choosing between food, gas, or a bus ticket to get to work, necessary clothing, and the rising cost of utilities. According to many residents and businesses the water bills have been rising over the years in an attempt, some believe, to push poor African American residents out of the city of Detroit to make room for other more acceptable residents who can afford the higher water prices and to allow for the privatization of water.

In her own words, the Samaritan woman testified that Jesus "told me everything I have ever done." Readers who continue to read this statement as referring only to the woman's previous and present domestic situations make her marital and/or sexual history "everything" relevant to her story. But what Jesus did was to take time to hear her full story. There is no part of the woman's story that Jesus condemns. Of course, too many women have internalized a patriarchal, sexist understanding of their lives that considers a woman's sexuality and sexual history and behavior as the sum of a woman's life and the test of her (im)morality. We are not told "everything" that Jesus said to the women or that she shared with him, just like the author of John did not have sufficient space to write all that Jesus said and did (21:25). Through their dialogue, it is concluded that they worship the same God; that the worship of God transcends human habitations. Consistent with the chapter's opening statement that Jesus has not baptized anyone, he does not subject the woman to baptism, nor does he command her to repent of anything (4:2). Jesus did not even attempt to "convert" the Samaritan woman to his "religious" understanding of Jerusalem as the City

66. Ibid.

of Zion and the Temple of Jerusalem as the only place to worship God. Instead he seems to recognize that, "religion" is human-made and what God requires is that God's people worship God in spirit and in truth, which transcends tradition, buildings, and dogmas. The most significant revelation in this text and given their shared context, is the free offer from God of living water, access to which no person can live without and without which no person can experience life abundantly (10:10).

CHAPTER THREE

Race, Gender, and The Politics Of "Sass"

Reading Mark 7:24–30 Through a Womanist Lens of Intersectionality and Inter(con)textuality[1]

On July 10, 2015, Sandra Bland, a twenty-eight-year-old black female activist, was stopped by a Texas trooper for allegedly switching lanes without signaling. Three days after her controversial arrest, Texas authorities claimed that Sandra Bland hanged herself in her Waller County jail cell.[2] Many people on social media, across race, gender, and class, blamed Ms. Bland for her own death, arguing that she had the audacity to sass or talk back to a police officer. For some people, it is acceptable for people of color and black women in particular to be illegally detained, tried on the streets, and executed in our jails for sassing or talking back to a trooper or police officer. Therefore, black women's sass is viewed as a capital offense and of having no intrinsic value or meaning.

---

1. This chapter is reprinted here with permission of the copyright holder. It was originally published as Mitzi J. Smith, "Race, Gender, and the Politics of 'Sass': Reading Mark 7:24–30 Through a Womanist Lens of Intersectionality and Inter(con)textuality," in *Womanist Interpretations of the Bible: Expanding the Discourse, eds.* Gay L. Byron and Vanessa Lovelace (Atlanta: Society of Biblical Literature Press, 2016) 95–112.

2. Sanchez, "What We Know About the Controversy in Sandra Bland's Death."

In this chapter I read the story of the Syrophoenician woman (Mark 7:24–30; cf. Matt 15:21–28) through a womanist hermeneutical lens of sass (sometimes referred to as talk-back).[3] I interpret a biblical text as a black woman who embodies sass. Womanist sass is a legitimate contextual language of resistance. It is a mother tongue, a subversive, defiant, grown woman's speech. It is also what Mikhail Bakhtin calls *heteroglossia* (a "social diversity of speech types").[4] I read with sass and embody sass as an African American womanist biblical scholar who, like other women of color and women generally, has been labeled as "argumentative" and sassy by men and women alike, simply for persistently expressing a desire to know more than is "good" for a black woman to know, seeking clarification, or refusing to be silenced and dismissed. As a sassy womanist biblical scholar, I construct dialogue inter(con)textually, critically engaging and sassing/talking back to the story of the Syrophoenician woman. I also construct a dialogue between my readings of the biblical text and talk-back derived from the black community, including the talk-back of Maya Angelou, Audre Lorde, bell hooks, Frantz Fanon, and Ta-Nehisi Coates.

A WOMANIST LENS: BLACK WOMANISH SASS

According to Alice Walker a "womanist" is a woman of color who speaks and acts *womanish*. She behaves and talks like a grown and capable woman who assumes responsibility for her own well-being, and she is "committed to the survival and wholeness of entire people, male *and* female."[5] A womanist's commitment is manifest in her audacious, vocal, and vociferous pursuit of justice and freedom from disease and oppression. Silence in the face of injustice and oppression can be complicit in those very forces and systems that diminish life and wholeness while giving the illusion of survival. A womanist understands her survival and freedom to be interconnected with the well-being of the community. Sassy women who talk back to systemic injustice and oppression know these truths. Like Harriet Tubman, Sojourner Truth, Shirley Chisholm, Angela Davis, and so many others before her, Sandra Bland embodied a black womanish sass; she spoke

3. I chose Mark's version of the story because it is the shorter earlier version, and it emphasizes the power of the Syrophoenician woman's word (*logos*) as opposed to Matthew who explicitly emphasizes her faith, presumably in Jesus.

4. Bakhtin, "Discourse in the Novel," 253.

5. Walker, "Womanist," xi.

and acted womanish. Texas authorities called her "argumentative and uncooperative."[6] Sandra's mother believes Sandra "should be remembered . . . as an "activist, sassy, smart . . . she knew her rights."[7]

A womanist prioritizes and highly values black women's epistemology (ways of knowing), agency, experiences, lives, and artifacts, rather than accepting them as peripheral to white feminist thought. Womanism centers black women as forethought and not as a theoretical addendum or critically provoked afterthought of white women's and black men's collective political awakening, activism, and God-talk. Womanism is feminism's sister and not its child. Black women's proto-womanism was seldom televised or legitimized, except, for example, in writing their autobiographies. Yet black women have always been improvising and creating as well as resisting slavery, lynching, disenfranchisement, racism, sexism, classism, sexual violence, and other oppressions inflicted upon black women, the black community, and others. Womanism, as a political movement, seeks to eradicate hegemonic interlocking systems of oppression, including sexism, classism, and racism, and their impact on the lives of black women and their communities.

For black women, talk-back and/or sass has been and remains in some situations the only means of agency, of being heard and of combating an other-imposed invisibility; it is resistance language that children, women, people of color, and black women in particular, speak and embody, inside and outside black communities and institutions. Sass is often defined as mouthing off, talking back, back talking, attitude, a woman not backing down to a man, or a child determined to have the final word in response to a real or perceive injustice or wrong. A sassy person is said to be impudent and insolent and is regarded as one who fails to show another person, a presumed superior, the respect or submissive behavior he or she has been socialized to expect within patriarchal systems, normally served up with so-called "arrogance" and "rudeness." Wives, children, slaves, and others of inferior social or economic standing can be guilty of sassing their husbands or significant others, fathers, masters, patrons, or employers.

The term is usually applied to the behavior of persons considered inferior or subordinate, by race, gender, position, class, or age to the person toward whom the talk, back talk, gesture and/or attitude is addressed. Black

6. Sanchez, "What We Know."
7. Silva, "Sandra Bland's Mother Speaks Out."

feminist scholar bell hooks defines "back talk" or "talking back" as "speaking as an equal to an authority figure . . . daring to disagree . . . having an opinion."[8] Sass or talk-back can refer to verbal and nonverbal behaviors, like placing one's hands on one's hips, rolling one's eyes. A person can sass, be sassy, or talk back without saying a word, by simply doing the opposite of what is expected or asked of him or her and in an in-your-face sort of way.

I use sass or talking back interchangeably, since sass consists of verbal and nonverbal gestures of defiance and resistance. Sass is when the oppressed name, define, call out, and sometimes refuse to submit to oppressive systems and behaviors. More specifically it is black women's refusal to remain silent about, or in the face of, oppression and violence committed against black women's bodies and minds and their families and communities.[9]

During slavery, Jim Crow, and the disenfranchisement of black people, it was expected that black people and women would happily defer to all white people regardless of age, gender, and position. Some believe this societal norm should never have changed; that sass or being sassy is never appropriate behavior for black people when directed at white people, even if one holds the most powerful office in the world. Ariana Dickey's comment about President Obama's appearance on the Internet talk show "Between Two Ferns" is at least reminiscent of a past and its refusal to die. Dickey wrote, "and boy, did Obama sass Zach [Galifianakis] back."[10]

Sass or talk-back are unacceptable behavior when directed at men, particularly white men. The "Opie and Andy" radio talk show posted a video entitled "Sassy Fat Black Girl Witness at Trayvon Martin Trial," in which Gregg "Opie" Hughes and Anthony Cumia berated nineteen-year-old Haitian-American Rachel Jeantel's hair, weight, physiognomy (lips, eyes), sexuality, "incoherent" speech (her *heteroglossia*), and her audacity (in their eyes) to become angry, frustrated, and finally to talk back to the prosecutor during her testimony.[11] Apparently, Ms. Jeantel's race, class, and gender made her sass even more unpalatable and intolerable at best and an object of comedic humiliation at worst.

8. hooks, *Talking Back*, 5.

9. Stover, "Nineteenth-Century African American Women's Autobiography," 133–54.

10. Dickey, "Obama 'Between Two Ferns.'"

11. Opie and Andy, "Sassy Fat Black Girl Witness."

"Sass" is an Americanism; it is slang created in the context of a patriarchal, gendered, and racialized society. America has always been and remains a racialized, patriarchal society. Yet the black woman, as the subject of Maya Angelou's poem "Still I Rise," survives and thrives despite the history of lies and oppression that objectify and demonize her; her rising is a talking back and sass/sassy. The second verse of that poem begins with the first of a series of rhetorical questions: "Does my sassiness upset you?/ why are you beset with gloom?/cause I walk like I've got oil wells/ pumping in my living room."[12] Angelou's poem, dedicated to her mother, Vivian Baxter, is sass/talk-back and testifies about the experience of many other sassy black women who preceded her and follow her. The poem's rhetorical questions imply that the black woman's oppressors would rather see her broken and submissive ("bowed head and lowered eyes") than sassy and haughty. She rises as "the dream and hope of the slave" abandoning the past, its terror and fear.[13]

In reading Mark's story of the Syrophoenician Woman (7:24–20; cf. Matt 15:21–28) through a womanist lens of sass, I examine this sassy woman and her speech as *heteroglossia*. Bakhtin defines *heteroglossia* as the broad range and possibilities of "social diversity of speech types" embedded in a narrative through the speech of characters, narrators, authorial voice, and genres.[14] The Syrophoenician woman's speech represents a social diversity; it is a culturally determined and subversive improvisation. I read her speech as resistance language. It is a contextual, subversive mother tongue. I read as a sassy woman talking back to the text from a place of anger and pain at the senseless deaths of black women like Sandra Bland and Natasha McKenna who sassed and died.[15] I read in remembrance of the sassy black women who preceded Bland and McKenna. And I read also with those oppressed women who could not muster the courage to be sassy, to talk back to their oppressors and oppressions. I also "read darkness," which is "viewing and experiencing the world in emergency mode, as through the individual and collective experience of trauma."[16] I stand in solidarity with

12. Angelou, "Still I Rise," 7.

13. Ibid., 8, 9.

14. Bakhtin, "Discourse in the Novel," 263.

15. Natasha McKenna was an African American woman diagnosed with schizophrenia, who died in police custody after being shocked four times with a stun gun. Weil, "Death of Woman."

16. Wimbush, "Introduction: Reading Darkness," 21.

Sandra Bland. I read because of her and other sassy womanists. Knowing Sandra Bland's story has changed me in the way that the murder of Ta-Nehisi Coates's friend Prince Jones, killed by a Prince George's County police officer, changed him: "The entire episode took me from fear to a rage that burned in me then, animates me now, and will likely leave me on fire for the rest of my days. . . . My response was, in this moment, to write."[17]

I read the story of the Syrophoenician woman intentionally as a black woman, consciously aware of my solidarity with Sandra Bland, Natasha McKenna, and with black women before her who have experienced the same or a similar fate and those after her whose stories will be read similarly. I read knowing that my sisters, nieces, nephews, brothers, and other family and community members could face a fate similar to these black women. We might, at any time, resist our oppressor, our oppression as sassy black women, but we might not survive.

BORDER CROSSINGS: PLACE, RACE, AND GENDER

Before she died, Sandra Bland had relocated from Chicago to Texas, having accepted a position at her alma mater, Prairie View A&M University. In Texas, Sandra Bland planned to continue her work as an activist in support of Black Lives Matter (BLM). Chicago is a city plagued by violence, but it was in Waller County, Texas, which is infamous for a different kind of violence, where Sandra Bland was so unfortunate to be stopped. Former Waller County Judge DeWayne Charleston describes Waller County as "the most racist county in the state of Texas which is probably one of the most racist states in the country."[18] Hempstead, a city in Waller County, still has separate cemeteries for white and black residents. Between 1882 and 1968 Mississippi had the highest lynchings with 581; Georgia was second with 531, and Texas was third with 493.[19] Violence, racism, sexism, and other forms of oppression transcend boundaries.

Such boundaries are evident in how Jesus moves from place to place in his ministry in the Gospel of Mark. Although this is the first time in Mark's narrative that Jesus himself crosses over into Tyre (7:24), people from Tyre and Sidon had come to him in Galilee for healing (3:7–8). Once word traveled that Jesus was healing people of diverse illnesses and casting

17. Coates, *Between the World and Me*, 82.
18. Toh, "Sandra Bland Death."
19. Chestnutt, "Lynching Statistics."

out demons or unclean spirits, the crowds seeking his help increase exponentially. The people whom Jesus healed from Tyre and Sidon likely went back home. And maybe it is in the home of someone whom Jesus previously healed that he finds refuge. This is the first time Jesus enters a house for the purpose of being alone. At other times Jesus sought relief and respite from the press of the crowds, but he never successfully avoided people or the crowds in anybody's house. Why should this house be any different just because it is in Tyre?

In this house in Tyre, Jesus's disciples are conspicuously absent from the narrative (cf. Matt 15:23, where the disciples are present in the house and aggressively oppose the Canaanite woman). Perhaps Jesus thought that by crossing the border into Tyre he could finally escape the crowds, that people would not be so needy. But people need help and deliverance from unclean spirits on both sides of the border. The human need for wholeness transcends borders; it transcends gender, sexuality, race/ethnicity, and class. The reader has been prepared for the resolution of the tension created by Jesus' desire to escape notice.

What is different about this place is Jesus' encounter with a solitary woman who locates Jesus despite his desire to be left alone. The narrator does not think it significant to inform his readers how the woman gained entry into the house, or whether she experienced resistance at the door. Mark does not say whether the master of the house is Jewish, Gentile, part Jewish and part Gentile (like Timothy, Acts 16:1), Godfearer, or what? Maybe it does not matter. Racial and gender biases are impactful and efficacious when practiced by people who have power and authority to limit or deny access to resources. We know that somehow the Syrophoenician woman gains an audience with Jesus, but we don't know whether the interaction takes place inside or outside of the house. But this place, Tyre, should be neutral and friendly territory for her. It is either home or close to home. But oppressions, like sexism, racism, and classism, transcend place and transgress borders because defiled, fallible human beings are carriers of oppression, and Jesus is no exception.

Mark's Jesus enters and exits houses, but each threshold tells a new story. The narrator explicitly informs his readers that the woman who finds Jesus is Greek (*Hellēnis*). Many Greeks in Palestine and southern Syria shared collective identities that distinguished them from Jewish people (and vice versa). Nathanael Andrade asserts that, "despite their internal ethnic and cultural disparities, the citizen bodies of Iamnia, Caesarea, Scythopolis, and other such cities constituted Greek collectivities, to be distinguished from Jewish ones."[20] Jewish people claimed certain civic states as their own based on the previous conquest of Greek cities, like Tyre under the Hasmonaeans, despite subsequent Roman colonization. Syria was annexed to Rome in 64 BCE and Judea the previous year in 63 BCE. Prior to Roman annexation, the Hasmonaeans had conquered both Syria and Phoenicia.[21]

More precisely, the woman is racially a Syrophoenician; she is possibly mixed race. In the first century BCE and CE "the terms Greek and Syrian could be used to describe intersecting civic categories, not mutually exclusive ethnic ones."[22] While the term *Greek* could describe the Syrophoenician woman's language, "it is just as possible that it framed her in civic terms as a gentile member of a Greek polity, whether she spoke Greek or a near Eastern language," such as Aramaic.[23] "As a Tyrian, she belonged to what by [Mark's] lifetime were the regional *koinon* or *eparchaeia* of Phoenicia (or Tyre), the Syrian *ethnos*, and the Greek city-state of Tyre, which was of course Phoenician by origin."[24]

The woman is impure in relation to Jesus. Jesus is what she is not, a Jewish man. In the immediate narrative context (7:1–23), Jesus had previously taught his disciples at someone's house. He taught them it is not what goes into the body that defiles a person, but it is what comes out of him that defiles (7:14–23). Did this teaching only apply to hand washing and food or does it apply to people as well (cf. Acts 10:28)?

The other thing that we are told about the woman is that she has a daughter with an unclean spirit. This Greek Syrophoenician woman bears a triple stigma because of her race, gender, and as the mother of a demon-possessed daughter. Like African American women and other women of color she experiences racism, sexism, and classism as interlocking forms of oppression. All three forms of oppression are highlighted in the narrative and they impact how Jesus responds to the woman.

In Mark, the diagnosis of being demon possessed or having an unclean spirit seems to be a blanket category. An unclean spirit is a stubborn visitor that will not willingly leave the body it has called home; it will throw a temper tantrum when commanded to leave (3:26); unclean spirits recognize

20. Andrade, "Ambiguity, Violence, and Community," 370.

21. Koester, *Introduction to the New Testament*, 208–10.

22. Andrade, "Ambiguity, Violence, and Community," 353.

23. Ibid., 254.

24. Ibid., 354.

Jesus and each call him by a different name or title (Holy one of God, and Son of the Most High God, 1:24; 5:7). Perhaps, the labeling of someone as demon possessed was a way of explaining behavior that was otherwise considered abnormal, objectionable, and threatening. For example, when Jesus went home to get a break from the overwhelming crowds, the crowds were so needy and intrusive that he couldn't even enjoy a meal with his family (3:19–20). Exhausted and unable to get a break from the overwhelming crowds, Jesus reacted in a human way; his family had to constrain him (3:21). Consequently, some wondered whether he had lost his mind, accusing Jesus of having an unclean spirit (3:30), a demon like the one's he had been exorcising from other folks (3:23). This Syrophoenician woman's daughter, like Jesus, has been diagnosed as having an unclean spirit. Impurity is socially constructed. What is constructed can be deconstructed.

Significantly, Jesus never touches people that are said to have unclean spirits; they are the untouchables. Jesus touches a leper who is considered unclean but his uncleanliness is not viewed as demon possession (1:40–41). The only person with an unclean spirit that Jesus touches is the boy from whom the disciples failed to exorcise the demon; however, it is only after the unclean spirit is expelled that Jesus touches the corpse (9:14–29). Even a corpse is touchable, but not people with unclean spirits.

It is out of ignorance that people are labeled as having "unclean spirits," as demon possessed because society finds something about their behavior unacceptable, abnormal, distasteful, threatening; they are out of order and different. Mary Douglas puts it this way: "where there is dirt there is system";[25] there is a normal way of being and behaving. We can respond to perceived anomalies in two ways. We can ignore them as if they don't exist or we can acknowledge their existence and condemn them.[26]

In relation to Jesus, the woman as a Syrophoenician experiences triple stigmatization even in her own neighborhood. She has no ontological existence outside of her colonized, racialized, and othered group identity. Frantz Fanon wrote that, "every ontology is made unattainable in a colonized and civilized society. . . . In the *Weltanschauung* of a colonized people there is an impurity, a flaw that outlaws any ontological explanation. . . . Ontology—once it is finally admitted as leaving existence by the wayside—does not permit us to understand the being of the black man [or woman]

25. Douglas, *Purity and Danger*, 36.
26. Ibid., 39.

. . . the black man [or woman] has no ontological resistance in the eyes of [white people]."[27]

THE POLITICS AND POWER OF SASS

The Syrophoenician woman bowed and begged for Jesus' attention and help. But Jesus responded to her deference and her submissiveness with these words: "Permit the children (*tekna*) to be fed first, for it is not good (*kalos*) to take the bread from the children (*tekna*) and to throw it to the dogs," 7:27 (my translation). Jesus responded to her in a way that betrayed his Jewish male bias. As Emerson Powery states, Jesus has triply marginalized this woman: She is female, a Greek, non-Jewish foreigner, and she is, if implicitly, a dog.[28] In Jesus' reasoning, to give bread to the dogs requires taking it from the children; that to give food to the "dogs" will result in short changing the children who deserve priority. In other words, "all lives matter," despite the fact that all people do not experience disease and oppressions to the same degree as others. In this moment, the mother pleading the imminent, urgent case of her sick child should matter most. (The slogan "all lives matter" in response to "black lives matter" dismisses the impact of racism on people of color in a racialized society.) The woman is likened to the "dogs" that have no place at the table. Generally, ancient Semitic peoples did not care for dogs as household pets.[29] If there happens to be any leftovers they will be thrown at her, like a dog in an alley. She must behave like a Greek, a Syrophoenician and a woman in relation to this Jewish man. She is impure and subordinate to Jewish people, despite their shared geopolitical status as colonized peoples. Fanon writes, "I was expected to behave like a black man—or at least like a nigger" while a man should behave like a man.[30] Similarly black women must be black women in relation to white men. In a racialized society, black women are not viewed

27. Fanon, *Black Skins, White Masks*, 109–10.

28. Powery, "The Gospel of Mark," 136.

29. Lazenby, "Greek and Roman Household Pets," 245; see Gosling, "Pets in Classical Times," 109–13. This does not mean that all Semitic peoples shared the same negative feeling toward dogs as household pets any more than one could say all Greeks and Romans, without exception, loved dogs as pets and welcomed them under their tables. The story of the rich man and Lazarus implies the presence of dogs under the rich man's table; the dogs lick Lazarus' wounds as he hopes to catch some of the crumbs that fall from the table (Luke 16:21).

30. Fanon, *Black Skins, White Masks*, 114.

and treated as women on equal footing with white women. Black women's skin color trumps their gender; they are seen and treated as black persons first and secondarily as flawed females inferior to white women. Sojourner Truth so poignantly responded to this racist ideology in her "Ain't I a Woman" speech (at a Women's Rights Convention in Akron Ohio in 1851), disrupting, with her sass and back talk, the racist ideology that questioned her womanhood because of her race and her former enslavement. With thunderous voice, Truth asserted that nothing she experienced or that was withheld from her nullified or changed the fact of her identity as a woman.

Jesus' words signify a tradition and ideology of racial priority, an "un-reasoned" reason, justifying his denial of the woman's request. The woman can either submit to her oppression or she can challenge and resist affirming her own humanity. Colonization does not encourage unity among the colonized; it encourages them to guard the crumbs. The oppressed are expected to achieve wholeness on the crumbs, to be treated like dogs and yet remain civil and silent.

But the Syrophoenician woman will not be silenced; she will resist. She resists this triple marginalization with her *logos*, her word, her sass; she draws upon "inner resources" left to the reader's imagination.[31] She resists as a woman, as a mother with a sick child. Jesus invoked a text, an oppressive text—oppressive for mother and child. So the woman resists with sass and talk-back: "she answered and said to him, 'Master even the household table dogs eat from the crumbs of the children (*paidia*)," (7:28; my translation). I propose that the noun "crumbs" metonymically signifies the children's plates. In the woman's sass, the dogs don't have to wait until the children are fed first; the dogs are treated with compassion as beloved household pets. Many ancient Greeks and Romans, unlike many Semitic peoples generally, did not abhor animals like dogs but welcomed them into their houses. In fact, dogs and other animals were "dedicated to gods or goddesses."[32] Homer's *Iliad* mentions "dogs I raised in my halls to be at my table" and "nine dogs of the table that had belonged to the lord Patroklos."[33] As early as 600 BCE ancient vase paintings show dogs in houses under tables. Rich and poor alike loved their dogs. An ancient Gallic relief depicts "a boy reclining on a couch and giving his pet dog his plate to lick clean."[34]

31. Powery, "The Gospel of Mark," 136.
32. Lazenby, "Greek and Roman Household Pets," 245.
33. Homer, *The Iliad*, 22.69; 23.173.
34. Lazenby, "Greek and Roman Household Pets," 246.

Because of the woman's experiences, her context as a Greek, Syro-phoenician woman, she embodies sass from her unique epistemological context. Her sass is *heteroglossia*. The woman resists with the only thing she has, her reason (*logos*), her sass; she was up against something unreasoned. "For a man whose only weapon is reason there is nothing more neurotic than contact with unreason."[35] To be despised because of one's race (gender, sexuality, or class) is to be "up against something unreasoned."[36]

The fact that we can seek liberation from one form of oppression while thoroughly entrenched in another is the beast of socialization absent con-scientization. Surekha Nelavala argues that the woman in her response to Jesus says "yes" but "no"; she plays it smart by "pretending she was accept-ing" Jesus' argument and used it to her own advantage and by not behaving as if Jesus insulted her.[37] But the woman's deference to Jesus demonstrated by her addressing him as master would be typical behavior of most women socialized in a patriarchal society. Besides, her initial genuflecting and pleading do not result in a positive outcome, but an oppressive word.

The Syrophoenician woman did not let the differences in their ethnic-ity or status, Jesus' reputation as a healer, or any stigma associated with her having a daughter possessed by an unclean spirit hinder her from sassing or talking back to Jesus. She questioned Jesus and the authoritative tradition he quoted that could have stopped her in her tracks and denied her daugh-ter the healing she sought and needed, and which he had so freely bestowed upon others. Clearly, all lives don't matter equally. Jesus had no right to treat her as less than a dog in her hour of motherly desperation. Her life matters; her daughter's life matters—at least as much as the "dogs under the table." Syrophoenician lives matter! Syrophoenician women's lives matter!

The Syrophoenician woman went toe to toe with Jesus. The woman "uses his own argument."[38] "More than anything else, the personal narra-tives that formerly enslaved black women wrote are products of their re-sistance to various oppressions, and each writer uses the language of the oppressor to express that resistance."[39] The woman counters Jesus' speech with her *heteroglossia*. She engages in subversion and improvisation: (1) she speaks from her own cultural context, recontextualizing and substituting

35. Fanon, *Black Skins, White Masks*, 118.

36. Ibid.

37. Nelavala, "Smart Syrophoenician Woman," 68.

38. Dewey, "The Gospel of Mark," 485.

39. Stover, "Nineteenth-Century African American Women's Autobiography," 137.

Jesus's words with her sass. In her sass, *tekna* becomes *paidia*. In her sass, her people sit at the table; (2) the *paidia*, unlike the *tekna*, demonstrate compassion for the table dogs, allowing them to eat crumbs off their plates; and (3) she eliminates the language of priority. "An African American vernacular has always been recognized as a black way of speaking, and like all vernaculars, it grew out of a need to speak subversively, to speak in a 'language' that was shared by other members of one's 'community' but that confounded those outside of it."[40]

Significantly, Jin Young Choi argues that the Syrophoenician woman "embodies tactic." However, I disagree with Choi's assertion that it is the "art of the weak;"[41] it is more complex. Given this cultural linguistic shift, the Syrophoenician woman has flipped the script. It is *heteroglossia*.[42] With *paidia*, hers is a mother's tongue or language for her people and her child. Stover argues that, "African American forms of expression such as black folktales, signifying, playing the dozens, and an infinite variety of subversive use of language—sass, invective, impudence, back talking, just to name a few—demonstrate Bakhtin's *heteroglossia* criteria, forming the base for what I call an African American 'mother tongue.'"[43] bell hooks writes that in her community where she grew up in the south talking back was risky and daring and satisfied the craving (or need) to "have a voice, and not just any voice but one that could be identified as belonging to" her.[44] The Syrophoenician woman improvises at the axis of her need and Jesus' denial, constructing her own *heteroglossia*, a language that resists oppression and claims her own humanity.

Jesus' consciousness is raised as a result of the woman's sass. Mark's Jesus uses the grammatically neuter Greek noun *teknon* (child) when he addressed the man-child, whose friends lowered him through the roof so that Jesus might heal him (2:5). Mark's Jesus used *teknon* the second time in this conversation with the Syrophoenician woman to refer to the Jewish people (7:27). In between these two instances of *teknon*, we find one occurrence of the Greek noun *paidion* (child) referring to Jairus's fatally ill daughter (*thugatarion*) whom Jesus resurrects (5:39). Perhaps, when Mark's Jesus calls Jairus' daughter (*thugatarion*) a *paidion*, it signifies her putative

40. Ibid., 140.

41. Choi, *Postcolonial Discipleship of Embodiment*, 94.

42. Bakhtin, "Discourse in the Novel," 262–67.

43. Stover, "Nineteenth-Century African American Women's Autobiography," 139.

44. hooks, *Talking Back*, 5.

subordinate status as a female. She is an outsider belonging to an insider (Jairus).

The Syrophoenician woman's sass mattered, tugging at and tapping into Jesus's humanity and compassion. She was an advocate and an activist for her child and for other mothers and their children who could be denied justice and wholeness based on biased traditions and Rabbis who have been socialized to value those traditions. The Syrophoenician mother challenged what Jesus labeled good or fair (*kalos*, 7:27). That is what sass does; it challenges those systems, traditions, and people that are neither just nor moral, but deleterious and deadly to one's self, one's people, and to the human race. "Moving from silence into speech is for the oppressed, the colonized, the exploited, and those who stand and struggle side by side a gesture of defiance that heals, that makes new life and new growth possible. It is . . . the liberated voice."[45]

After Jesus' encounter with her, Mark's Jesus uses *paidion* as a more inclusive term. He embraces a *paidion* and admonishes that anyone who welcomes any *paidion* like this one welcomes him and God (9:36–37). Also after his encounter with the Syrophoenician woman, people bring their children (*paidion*) to him; it is such children (*paidion*) as these to whom the kingdom of God belongs (10:13–16). Jesus only reverts to *teknon* when speaking directly to his circle of disciples, referring to them as *teknon* (10:24, 28; cf. 12:18–21 where *teknon* is put into mouth of Sadducees; 13:12).

IT IS BECAUSE OF YOUR WORD (*LOGOS*)/SASS

In response to the woman's sass, Jesus acknowledges the power of her word (*logos*) and her reasoning. Choi acknowledges that it is the woman's *logos* that engenders healing for her daughter, but she further asserts that the woman consumes the crumbs partaking of the mystery of Jesus' body.[46] In Mark, when Jesus casts a demon or unclean spirit out of an individual, the language is clear that Jesus has cast out the demon/unclean spirit (1:21–28, 34; 3:21–28; 6:13; 9:25). These exorcisms are expressed with the Greek verb *ekginomai* in the second aorist imperative when Jesus is the agent (3:25; 5:8; 9:25), with the Greek verb *ekballō* when the narrator or other characters refer to Jesus's exorcism activities in the third person (1:34; 3:22, 23); or when Jesus commissioned the twelve apostles to perform exorcisms, the

45. Ibid., 9.

46. Choi, *Postcolonial Discipleship of Embodiment*, 100.

present infinitive of *ekballō* occurs (3:15; cf. 6:13), usually translated "cast out." In Caesarea Philippi, despite Jesus having given his apostles power over unclean spirits, they were unable to expel the spirit from a young boy (9:17–18), which suggests being one of Jesus' followers and being commissioned by him does not guarantee successful exorcisms. The twelve apostles were disturbed that in Capernaum somebody who was not one of them was casting out demons in Jesus' name (9:38–41; cf. Luke 9:49–50). Mark demonstrates that perceived others/outsiders can exorcise demons or unclean spirits; I argue that this Syrophoenician woman becomes one of them. When she seeks Jesus' help for her daughter, she does not know the power of her sass, but she is about too.

Here Jesus says, "on account of this word (*logos*), go [home]; the demon has gone out of your daughter" (7:29). He does not command the demon to leave, but directs the sassy mother to go home. Jesus knows that the demon has left her child's body. Nelavala argues that Jesus has been transformed; that this is "the miracle" when the oppressed can "persuade their oppressor for a change."[47] The assertion that, "without the oppressor's readiness to change, the voice of the oppressed is in vain"[48] contributes to a hopelessness that too many oppressed feel, a hopelessness that keeps too many away from the ballot box and assures complicity in their own oppression.

In his book, *Between the World and Me,* Coates advises his son about the intrinsic value of struggle and resistance against oppression: "you are called to struggle, not because it assures you victory but because it assures you an honorable sane life."[49] Jesus simply affirms the power of this Greek Syrophoenician woman's sass. Her word, her sass, has power. But Jesus casts no spell; there is no *ekballō*. And the Greek syntax differs from the other Markan exorcism episodes. Jesus gives his twelve disciples the authority to cast out demons, but they don't; instead he affirms the authority embodied in this woman's sass. It is *her* word, *her* sass, that brings restoration and relief to her child. Her daughter is no longer one of the untouchables.

Sass gushes up from a place of pain and anger, of being "sick and tired of being sick and tired," of living with "unclean spirits" that claim one's body, mind, and soul. One might say, therefore, that it is truth-telling with an attitude, and for good reason. Sass explodes on the scene, talking back

---

47 Nelavala, "Smart Syrophoenician Woman," 68.

48 Ibid., 66.

49. Coates, *Between the World and Me,* 97.

to racism, sexism, classism, and other isms that persist and refuse to desist; that refuse to be expelled without leaving its mark on one's body, soul, and mind. The power of sass is the power of truth-telling, the power of breaking the silence that oppression inflicts upon its victims. Sass is often a woman's last resort. A sassy woman takes a risk, a possibly fatal risk, in confronting oppression. The last stanza in Audre Lorde's poem "A Litany for Survival" reads: "and when we speak we are afraid/our words will not be heard / nor welcomed / but when we are silent / we are still afraid / so it is better to speak /remembering / we were never meant to survive."[50] Women like Sandra Bland sass or talk back not because of the absence of fear, but because they know history and current events show that, "we were never meant to survive." But we use our "mother tongues," our sass and talk-back, for our children, at least hoping they will have a better life and not have to be constrained and demonized by the unclean spirits of racism, sexism, and classism.

Certainly, sass and talk-back can have fatal outcomes when the person to whom it is directed has more regard for unjust traditions or for his own ego and authority than for human freedom and life, as in the case of Sandra Bland and others. The biblical writers were selective regarding the stories they chose to preserve and narrate. Life is a lot messier and does not wrap up in tidy salubrious and felicitous denouements. The empire always strikes back. For unjust systems to fall, it takes a movement of women and men willing to sass and talk back, risking retaliation and even life. Unjust systems and the people who prosper from them don't just wake up one day and decide that they are tired of the benefits and implode. What we also know for sure is that the utter silence of the oppressed (and their supposed allies) will never topple the master's house.

The story of the Syrophoenician woman provides an antithesis to the silent submissive woman who dares not sass or talk back to male authority figures, regardless. This story can assist in constructing a more empowering and freeing theology of sass or talk-back that demonstrates the impact and value of women's sass or talk-back. The Syrophoenician woman stands in the tradition of biblical predecessors like Queen Vashti. Sandra Bland stood that fatal day in the tradition of proto-womanists like Ida Wells Barnett, Fannie Lou Hamer, Septima Clark, Rosa Parks, and other activists. However, she did not choose to be memorialized in a similar tragic fashion with Emmett Till, Miriam Carey, Natasha McKenna, Yvette Smith, Tanisha

50. Lorde, "A Litany for Survival," 32.

Anderson, Rekia Boyd, Kindra Chapman, and too many others who were murdered because of their race. The abuse and illegal arrest of Sandra Bland and subsequent attempts by Trooper Encinia and his department to cover up the "truth," at the very least precipitated her untimely and unnecessary death and at most constitutes a modern-day lynching (with a plastic bag and a large quantity of marijuana while in custody?!!). Bland would be alive today had Trooper Encinia not singled her out for harassment and escalated the situation because she dared to sass and talk back, to resist his oppressive ways.

Women continue to be taught that they are to be good "footstools" for men. When a woman "acts up" or refuses to be that footstool, a "biblically" submissive woman, then she deserves any violence inflicted upon her. Too many women remain shackled to this type of thinking and so they do all they can to be "good girls." (I even heard a female minister not long ago at a breast cancer event promoting the book she wrote about how women can be little girls again and thus become good marriage material), always submissive to male authority and abuse. And sass or talk-back are certainly not the qualities of submission.

The story of the Syrophoenician woman shows that sass can call our attention to and challenge unjust, biased, and oppressive traditions, laws, and expectations. The power of sass can reveal and question the destructive forces at work in or against our communities. Too often when many women of color have sassed or talked back, confronting unfair practices, biased policies, racist behaviors that they have witnessed or experience in church, society, or the academy, they have been labeled as trouble makers, castigated, marginalized, and ostracized by men as well as by their sister feminists and womanists. This practice of silencing the sass of women of color hinders womanism/feminism from being the political and self-critical movement it is meant to be. We need to celebrate sass and talk-back in women of color as well as in white women as a legitimate form of agency and method of truth telling rather than punishing women for speaking truth boldly in the face of corrupt, biased, life-threatening and denying authority. Sass and talk-back are legitimate forms of resisting oppression and exploitation. It can be considered a language ("mother tongue") of black women seeking to expose their exploitation and to dismantle the master's house built from and on the sands of racism, class, sexism, and domination. We must celebrate sassy sisters and tell their stories.

I travel alone for long distances relatively often. I am black and female. And on some days I am fed up, and I might just be courageous enough to assert my right to know, to be sassy, if I should be stopped by a cop. And that cop might be like Trooper Encinia. He might refuse to tell me why I am being stopped and yet expect my full unmitigated compliance. Or I might comply but be bullied and provoked—everyone, most people, have a breaking point. Like other black women and men in this country, my life could be cut short by one trivial, unnecessary encounter with the wrong police officer. Black people's fears are real. Sandra Bland, Kindra Chapman, Tamir Rice, Freddie Gray, and many others who died as a result of interactions with the police, in marked and unmarked graves, were real people who are mourned and missed by family and friends. For some it won't be real—the fear, the facts—until it happens to them or to someone they know. But now is past time to name and oppose this insidious brutality of people of color, women ,and men and demand "never again." #SayHerName #BlackWomensLivesMatter.

CHAPTER FOUR

Epistemologies, Pedagogies, and the Subordinated Other

Luke's Parallel Construction of the Ethiopian Eunuch and the Alexandrian Apollos (Acts 8:26–40; 18:24–28)[1]

Luke-Acts scholars have noted parallels and/or similarities between the Ethiopian eunuch and other biblical (e.g., Cornelius, the Elijah/Elisha tradition)[2] and extrabiblical (e.g., King Izates in Josephus's *Antiquities*)[3] characters. To my knowledge, however, scholars have not given any serious or sustained attention to parallels between the stories of Ethiopian Eunuch and the Alexandrian Jewish man, Apollos (8:26–40; 18:24–28). In

1. This essay is based on a paper presented at the 2015 Society of Biblical Literature Luke-Acts Section panel on characterization in Luke-Acts. I dedicate this chapter to my late dissertation advisor, mentor, colleague and friend Prof. Francois Bovon, an excellent Luke-Acts scholar and compassionate human being, who valued intuition for doing biblical interpretation.

2. See for example, Tannehill, *The Narrative Unity of Luke-Acts*, 110; Haenchen, *The Acts of the Apostles*; Jervell, *Die Apostelgeschichte*, 270–71; Dahl, "Nations in the New Testament." See also Burrus, "The Gospel of Luke and the Acts of the Apostles," 133–55; Gaventa (*From Darkness to Light*, 106) argues that the Ethiopian Eunuch is a symbolic convert; Martin ("A Chamberlain's Journey, at 177) states the eunuch is "symbolic" and yet is also a "partial fulfillment" of Acts 1:8; Williams, "Acts of the Apostles," 226; Dibelius, *Studies in the Acts of the Apostles*; Trocmé, *Le livre des Actes et l'histoire*; Spencer, *The Portrait of Philip in Acts*.

3. Josephus, *J. Ant.* 20.44–46.

this chapter, I argue that the narratives about the Ethiopian Eunuch and Apollos are parallel accounts that are connected rhetorically, ideologically, and geopolitically. Both characters are natives of countries on the African continent—Ethiopia and Egypt, respectively. Ethiopia and Egypt are often mentioned together in the Hebrew Bible as objects of conquest, of Israel's hope and boasting, and of ransom for Israel; each are places of wealth and nations from which Yahweh will recover his people (Isa 11:11, 20:3, 43:3, 45:14; cf. Nah 3:9). Traditionally, Egypt and Ethiopia have been both objects of fear and desire or fetish: "Thus says the LORD: The wealth of Egypt and the merchandise of Ethiopia, and the Sabeans, tall of stature, shall come over to you and be yours, they shall follow you; they shall come over in chains and bow down to you . . ." (Isa 45:14a, NRSV). That which we envy and desire, we often fear. I contend that Luke's inclusion of the two accounts about significant men of African descent demonstrates synecdochically the double marginalization and subordination of Alexandria and Ethiopia. The narrative constructions of both the Ethiopian eunuch and the Alexandrian Apollos support a particular way of knowing (epistemology) and of teaching (pedagogy) with regard to the "subordinated other" in an attempt to marginalize and subordinate the other in relation to a geo-political religious center.

I also read the two narratives inter(con)textually with the liberative pedagogies of African American women of color. As a part of this inter(con)textuality I insert my personal narrative. I am the only full-time tenured African American female professor in a predominantly white seminary teaching in one of its urban centers where my students are predominantly African American and female. I am also the only full-time tenured female in the biblical studies department and most often the only female teaching in my department. A scholarly personal narrative can "highlight authors' voices and share their perceptions and interpretation of their lived experiences," which can provide insights and perceptiveness often absent in research; it can constitute a "unique way to construct new knowledge."[4] A scholarly personal narrative integrates the individual's story with pertinent theories that assist in reflection; I integrate my personal narrative with liberative pedagogies. I also place my personal narrative in dialogue with the inter(con)textuality of the biblical text (and my interpretation of it) and the scholarship of women of color, particularly Katie Cannon and María del Carmen Salazar, together with the work of Paulo Freire on a liberative

4. Griffin, "Digging Deeper," 15. See also Nash, *Liberating Scholarly Writing*.

pedagogy. Salazar attempts to humanize her review of research on humanizing pedagogy by including her personal narrative and affirming the powerful potential of personal narrative for "illuminating and challenging the inhumanity that marks the oppressed."[5] From a womanist hermeneutical perspective I privilege the experiences of black women and other women of color that foreground womanist ways of knowing and pedagogy that are liberating. Katie Cannon states that a womanist pedagogy challenges "conventional and outmoded dominant theological resources, deconstructing ideologies that led us into complicity with our own oppression."[6]

I shall attempt to expose the ideologies operative in and across the two biblical narratives. The story of the Ethiopian eunuch can be understood as what I shall call a narrative double entendre: (a) it functions as a story of the conversion of the first Godfearer by a non-apostle paralleling the Cornelius household conversion narrative; conversely, the apostle Peter is instrumental in the latter; and (b) it also serves as a geopolitical and ideological parallel to the encounter between the wife and husband pair, Prisca and Aquila and the Alexandrian Jewish man Apollos. I focus on the latter. Different from Abraham Smith who argues that Acts 8:26–40 "functions as a part of Luke's critique and transformation of conventional understandings of power,"[7] I propose that Luke's stories of the Ethiopian eunuch and the Alexandrian Apollos function as both apologetic and subversive symbolic responses to the presence and power of the Roman Empire, demonstrating fetish and fear, envy and anxiety. I argue that Luke foregrounds the Ethiopian Eunuch's socio-economic capital demonstrated by his literacy, possessions, and connection with the Candace and her wealth, and he highlights Apollos's eloquence, as well as the provenance of both characters. Thus, in his characterization of each, Luke demonstrates his own fetish for and fear of the material and cultural capital that Rome highly valued.

Beyond the obvious geographical link between the Ethiopian Eunuch and Apollos—their African provenance, one being from the northern region and the other the interior region—a most haunting characterization is how Luke constructs them both as deficient in knowledge. Both are represented as deficient in certain knowledge and in need of instruction. However, more significant is the identity of the instructors and the manner and space in which the teachers instruct their African students. Both the

5. Salazar, "A Humanizing Pedagogy," 122.

6. Cannon, *Katie's Canon,* 137.

7. Smith, "A Second Step in African Biblical Interpretation," 214.

Ethiopian eunuch and Apollos are instructed by non-apostles who have recently been scattered or expelled from cities and forced to find refuge and do ministry in the margins. Unlike Theudas and Judas the Galilean whom Gamaliel mentions, the scattered non-apostles neither disappear nor die (5:33–39). Philip and Prisca/Aquila are Jewish believers that are forced out of Jerusalem/Judea and Rome, respectively. Prisca/Aquila are expelled from Rome and into Rome's colonized margins. Philip is forced out of Jerusalem and into the colonized Jewish diaspora. The last literary image left in the reader's mind when Philip and others are forced out of Jerusalem because of the persecution that followed Stephen's stoning, is the image of Paul, a Jewish Pharisee with Roman citizenship. Acts displays both Roman apologetic and subversive tendencies, attempts to appear politically innocuous to the Roman Empire, and also mitigates and subverts empire when *The Way* converts and subordinates those that represent or embody Roman values. Even those in the periphery of the center of authority in the Jesus movement and who are expelled by Rome are instrumental in converting or conquering those who embody wealth and social capital that Rome desires and fears. There is a fear of unbridled material and cultural capital, as well as a desire to conquer and incorporate such capital in *The Way*.

STRATEGIC ENCOUNTERS IN THE WAY

The encounters between Philip and the Ethiopian eunuch, and between Prisca and Aquila and Apollos differs from other orchestrated appointments in Acts that result in a conversion or the acceptance of a call (8:26–40; 18:24–28). In other extended narratives about individuals that experience a change of heart or convert to *The Way*, a meeting occurs between one individual and another (i.e., Saul and Ananias; Peter and Cornelius; Paul and Lydia and the jailer), when one or both parties receive a vision that directs them to a specific house or location. In some cases, both parties to the rendezvous receive visions (9:12; 10:3, 10; 11:5; 16:9–10). Differently, neither Philip, Prisca and Aquila, nor their students receive visions. Perhaps this is a part of the narrative's strategy that differentiates them from and subordinates them to the twelve apostles and to Paul, respectively. In Acts, it matters who teachers or leads whom.

Teaching and preaching can be anti-intellectual in Acts. The twelve apostles are described as "unlearned and ordinary" (4:13) and becoming an apostle or master-teacher does not require wisdom (1:20–22). Conversely, the Twelve select Philip and the other six Hellenists because they are "full of the Spirit and of wisdom" (6:3). Simultaneous with their election, the ministry of the Seven Hellenists is limited to table ministry, but the Twelve resolve to dedicate themselves to preaching the word of God; no table service for them (6:2)! When the subordinated Philip, a Spirit-filled, Sophia-filled, faith-filled, good man, is forced out of Jerusalem and Judea, he is exiled geographically and ministerially. He is exiled from Jerusalem as the headquarters of the movement and consequently from the table ministry in Jerusalem, which precipitates his encounter with the Ethiopian eunuch (and with Simon).

The angel of the Lord instructed Philip to leave Jerusalem and travel on the road (hodos) toward Gaza. The Ethiopian eunuch was already traveling on that road in his chariot. Consequently, when their paths providentially intersect, the Spirit directs Philip to approach the chariot. Approaching the Ethiopian eunuch's chariot, Philip hears the Ethiopian reading the book of Isaiah out loud. Similarly, Prisca and Aquila hear the eloquent Apollos speaking boldly in the synagogue (8:26–30; 18:26).

Philip pointedly questions the Ethiopian's ability to know (ginōskeis) for himself what he is reading (anaginōskeis), suggesting there is only one way to know the text (8:30). Perhaps the Ethiopian eunuch recognized Philip as a Hellenistic Jewish man. Who better to help him understand the Hebrew Scriptures? With humility, the Ethiopian eunuch responds by acknowledging his deficiency and the need for a guide (hodēgēsei) (8:31).[8] Philip does not function as a guide but as a witness like the Twelve. The Ethiopian was likely reading the Greek translation of the Scriptures (the Septuagint). Thus, unlike those at Pentecost who heard the wonderful works of God in their own languages (2:5–6), the Ethiopian attempts to understand the Scriptures in a foreign language, which is likely Philip's primary language. This is a cultural disadvantage for the Ethiopian, who probably spoke Ge'ez with Greek as a second language. The Isaiah text (53:7–8) that the eunuch is reading refers to an unidentified man using pronouns (he, his, him) and focuses on his slaughter, silence, humiliation, and death. The eunuch does not ask "why" the man suffers in silence, or why he is being humiliated and treated with violence. Luke depicts the Ethiopian eunuch as asking the right questions that solicit the right answers: Who is the

---

8. Judas failed as an apostolic witness but became a nefarious, treacherous guide (hodēgos) (1:16).

prophet talking about? Himself or someone else? (8:34). On the way and as a member of *The Way,* Philip explains to the Ethiopian the good news about Jesus (8:35). When the teacher and student riding in the Ethiopian's chariot arrive at a body of water, convinced of what he has been taught, the eunuch asks whether anything hinders Philip from baptizing him (Greek: *kōluō*) (8:37). (With Cornelius's conversion, it is Peter who asks if anything should prevent [*kōluō*] Cornelius and his household from being baptized, 10:47.) Both step down from the chariot and into the water where Philip baptizes the Ethiopian eunuch. And the Spirit carries Philip away (8:39–40).[9]

Although Prisca and Aquila engage in the same craft as Paul, they are clearly subordinate to Paul in terms of their ministry. The pair practice their tent making trade with Paul in Corinth. But when Paul teaches every Sabbath in the synagogue in Corinth, he appears to be a solo act the entire year and half (18:1–1). When Paul leaves for Syria the two accompany him, but he leaves them in Ephesus where they encounter Apollos in the synagogue preaching about Jesus with enthusiasm and accuracy (18:18–24). Apollos, a Jewish native of Alexandria, Egypt, is described as a man of eloquent words, very knowledgeable of the Scriptures, and instructed in *The Way of the Lord*. But after he preached, the eloquent Apollos who so accurately taught *the Way of the Lord* in the synagogue in Ephesus, is taken aside by Prisca and Aquila so they can teach him more accurately about *The Way of God*. Strategically, the phrase *The Way of God* only appears here in Acts (18:26), permitting some distinction, however slight, between what Apollos knew and what he lacked to warrant intervention in the margins. It is almost as if Luke needed to show, or maybe Luke felt his audience expected him to find a plausible reason to demonstrate that Apollos was deficient in knowledge. As Matthew Skinner correctly states, Apollos is described as having a "deficiency" of knowledge that is accurate but incomplete, knowing the baptism of John only.[10] The narrative implies that Apollos has no

---

9. Scholars have debated whether or not the Ethiopian eunuch was anointed by the Holy Spirit. The Western text contains a textual variant that reads: "the Holy Spirit fell on the eunuch, and the angel of the Lord caught up Philip" (TCGNT, 360). I would have previously argued that the Ethiopian eunuch was anointed because of the Spirit's guidance and presence at the scene, and that there is no evidence to show the eunuch did not receive the Holy Spirit or that his baptism was incomplete. See for example, Dunn, *Acts of the Apostles*, 115; Marshall, *Acts of the Apostles*, 157. However, I now think that Luke has intentionally slighted the Ethiopian eunuch as part of his strategy to subordinate the two characters of African descent, not because of their skin color but because of the wealth, military might, and wisdom connected with both.

10. Skinner, *Intrusive God, Disruptive Gospel,* 137.

knowledge of the baptism of the Spirit. And, as noted below, despite this scene, that epistemology gap is never closed! Prisca and Aquila taught him more accurately (*akribesteron*) about *The Way of God*, despite the fact that he accurately (*akribōs*) taught the Ephesians about Jesus (18:25, 28). Almost in the vein of a postscript, Luke wrote that Apollos knew only about John's baptism (18:25–26). Perhaps, just as the Romans left the task of teaching to capable slaves and freedpersons,[11] as their subordinates, the Twelve, for the most part, relegated teaching in the diaspora and the ministry of tables to their subordinates like Philip and Prisca and Aquila. Prisca, whose name is mentioned first, may have assumed the role of lead instructor when she and her husband school Apollos in *The Way of God*.[12] Perhaps, Prisca was a better teacher. Since both she and Aquila are subordinate to Paul, she is permitted to take the lead, a move that might have been intended to highlight the subordination of Apollos, an eloquent Jewish man from Alexandria, to a woman! Nevertheless, "they teach a teacher!"[13]

After Apollos had preached so eloquently in Ephesus, Paul returns and inquires as to whether the Ephesians had received the Holy Spirit; they were not even aware of the existence of the Holy Spirit (19:1–7). It seems that despite the fact that Prisca and Aquila rectified Apollos's supposed deficiency, neither teacher nor student laid hands on the Ephesians so that they might receive the Holy Spirit (19:6). Similarly, Philip was unable to lay hands on the Samaritans that he was instrumental in converting; Peter and John left Jerusalem to perform the anointing service (8:14–16).

Both the Ethiopian and the Alexandrian are literate (bilingual, knowledgeable, wise, and eloquent) and yet they are met in peripheral space and taught a singular orthodox way of reading, understanding, or knowing. The ignorance or deficiency of the Ethiopian and the Alexandrian is the subject of the narrative. After hearing Apollos speak boldly (and eloquently) in the synagogue, Prisca and Aquila pull him aside into spaced occupied only by the three of them in order to explain *The Way of God* more accurately to him.

As synecdochical symbols of Alexandria and Ethiopia, the eunuch and Apollos might be understood as objects of what Paulo Freire calls the "absolutizing of ignorance." The "absolutizing of ignorance" as a myth of oppressor ideology declares some as belonging to a group or class of people

11. Chiappetta, "Historiography and Roman Education," 152.

12. Fiorenza, *In Memory of Her*, 179.

13. Reimer, *Women in the Acts*, 210.

"who know or were born to know" and characterizes others as ignorant and "as alien entities"; the oppressor or dominant group decrees their own words as the only true words and it attempts to or succeeds in imposing them upon others.[14] Freire argues that revolutionary leaders reject the "absolutizing of ignorance" and will instead enter into dialogue with people. Domination is not the road to liberation.[15]

The mission among Jewish and Gentle audiences generally occurs in public settings (e.g., Pentecost festival, temple, synagogues,) or in households, but not on the road in a chariot or in a corner. The Apostles (primarily Peter and Saul/Paul) proclaim the good news to multitudes and to households resulting in conversions. However, in the case of the Ethiopian eunuch and the Alexandrian Apollos, two individual noteworthy characters from notable geopolitical places on the African continent, the non-apostles meet them in peripheral space, in the margins: The encounter between the Ethiopian eunuch and Philip occurs on an apparently scarcely traveled back road between Jerusalem and Gaza. As Brittany Wilson puts it "the eunuch and Philip are spatially 'betwixt and between': they are neither here nor there, but on a deserted road in the middle of the wilderness."[16] Both instances of instruction take place in private liminal out-of-the-way space indicative of the liminal (exiled) subordinate status of their teachers and a hegemonic and orthodox knowledge.

Both the Ethiopian eunuch and Apollos are exceptional and yet flawed. Both meet with marginalized characters in liminal space where didactic transformation takes place consummated by a ritual that does not effectively change their outsider status. Previously, Apollos had traveled freely, but afterwards he seems dependent on recommendation by the brothers for acceptance among the disciples. The Ethiopian eunuch needs no such endorsements because he is returning to Ethiopia. Like most, if not all, converts in Acts, the Ethiopian Eunuch and the Alexandrian Apollos are either god-fearing Gentiles, or Jewish. But they are the only characters who are characterized as participating in one-on-one instruction by marginal figures in the margins.

Neither the Ethiopian eunuch nor Apollos were invited to engage in dialogue about what they read or what they preached because the objective of their teachers is to indoctrinate them in *The Way.* Education that neglects

14. Freire, *The Pedagogy of the Oppressed*, 114–15.
15. Ibid., 108, 115.
16. Wilson, "'Neither Male nor Female,'" 418.

critical consideration of the world view of the student or the oppressed and does not reflect their locatedness in the world risks "preaching in the desert" or imposes a banking model that focuses on providing information to passive human receptacles.[17] Education as a practice of freedom cannot exist without critical dialogue in which students are teachers and teachers are students.[18]

Dialogue between students and teachers that values the prior knowledge that students bring to the learning process is the basis for a humanizing pedagogy. It also encourages critical engagement with others different from ourselves, not in order to dominate, but in pursuit of diverse dialogue partners. One way to incorporate and encourage student dialogue with persons different from themselves is through required readings that represent diverse voices and locatedness. Barbara Omolade asserts that, "the challenge of a Black feminist pedagogy is to use literature to connect people with ideas and histories across racial, gender, and class boundaries and to further connect Black women to each other and to their unique history."[19] Educators that value humanizing pedagogy will not be satisfied to simply supplement the majority malestream texts with minoritized voices, but will attempt to create equity by decentering androcentric and majority whitestream perspectives and concerns. Unfortunately, the majority introductory biblical studies textbooks present malestream and whitestream perspectives and, if the works of scholars of color are included, they are included in a way that further marginalizes their voices and/or contributions to the field. This marginalization is precisely why I no longer use an introductory text when I teach my Introduction to the New Testament course. It is necessary for minoritized scholars to think about writing introductory textbooks for biblical studies courses that decenter privileged whitestream and androcentric perspectives, voices, and concerns. Thus, an Asian-American male colleague and I are co-writing an introductory New Testament text in which we will attempt to privilege the concerns of communities of color and poor people and the scholarship of persons of color. Of the many publishers that turned down the book proposal for the text, one explicitly stated that they did not consider it an introductory text.

The privileging of voices of color and the concerns of communities of color in biblical studies, especially, but also in other seminary courses, is

17. Freire, *Pedagogy of the Oppressed*, 75, 77.

18. Ibid., 61–62.

19. Omolade, *The Rising Song of African American Women*, 133.

sometimes resisted or rejected not only by the academy but also by students of color who are not used to "hearing their own voices" (as one colleague put it). Students of color are accustomed to being taught by white male professors who privilege white male scholarship as the normative and legitimate voice. Most of my students are African-American females and most welcome the opportunity to engage the biblical text in their "own language," a "language" that is contextually relevant. Some students by their own accounts have stated that they have found their own voices in my biblical studies courses. Some students state that they will never view the biblical text the same way again. I take this to mean that they have learned to read the biblical text in more critically responsible ways that take seriously the contexts in which they live, work, and engage in ministry, even if they don't have the opportunity or courage to preach or teach in the ways they've learn to read. While I am too often impatient and disappointed when students are slow or fail to transfer what they learn to their ministry setting, I must remind myself that the first step is to have one's consciousness raised, to become aware that one does not have to read in ways that discount one's own voice and concerns, and those of our communities. Freire states that, "[l]iberation is a praxis; the action and reflection of men and women upon the world in order to transform it."[20] However, Freire also argues that action is sometimes impossible or not appropriate at a given moment; in those instances critical reflection is action.

Still some of my students are not sure that they are getting what they should from my courses; some think that they might be short changed in terms of mainstream biblical studies, despite the diversity of texts I use that include mainstream perspectives. New Testament and Old Testament courses are taught in alternating years in the Detroit Center. I am the only full-time professor in Detroit and the instructor designated to teach both testaments on a regular basis. Students may take courses online but most prefer the face-to-face classes. So as not to prolong completion of their programs, some students that completed my Spring 2017 Prophets course decided to take a summer intensive New Testament course in Ashland, Ohio, from one of my white male colleagues. One of those students stopped in my office and thanked me for preparing them well. She said they feel well prepared to take my colleague's course. They learned to construct and engage the historical, literary, and contemporary contexts and to critically reflect upon their own context as readers. They performed exegesis on texts

20. Freire, *Pedagogy of the Oppressed*, 60.

as individual interpreters, in small groups and as a class. We interrogated and problematized the biblical text and ideologies operative in texts. But we also privileged the concerns and voices of communities of color through required texts and in our discussions of current events. Yet students (and teachers) remain ambivalent wondering whether it is possible to privilege the voices and concerns of communities of color and also access mainstream biblical studies. According to Salazar, one principle and practice of humanizing pedagogy is teaching "students mainstream or dominant knowledge and discourse styles," for doing so, as an additive to "student's prior knowledge and discourse patterns," "provides students with 'insider' knowledge that is needed to successfully navigate the educational system."[21]

THE WAY AS AN EPISTEMOLOGICAL SITE OF HEGEMONIC TEACHING

The Way symbolizes one way of knowing, which is disseminated passively to those who would become members or insiders of *The Way*. Teaching is unilateral in Acts; it is not bilateral or dialogical. Either on *The Way*, in/about *The Way*, or both, implicitly and explicitly the Ethiopian eunuch and the Alexandrian Apollos are instructed in a particular way of reading or knowing. This unilateral, non-dialogical teaching occurs because both are depicted as deficient in their understanding or knowledge. In addition to their shared African provenance, the stories of the Ethiopian eunuch and the Alexandrian Apollos are connected in other ways. As noted, the Greek word *hodos* (translated either *road* or *way*) is present in and significant to both narratives. *The Way (hē hodos)* has spatial, ideological, and pedagogical implications that explicitly and implicitly connect both the Ethiopian Eunuch and the Alexandrian Apollos to their instructors: Philip explicitly teaches the Ethiopian on the road/way and implicitly in *The Way*; Prisca and Aquila pull Apollos aside and explicitly teach him *more accurately* about *The Way of God*. *The Way* designates a sect within Judaism that believes in Jesus as the Messiah. As a sect, it is said to be a ubiquitous object of antagonism (28:17–22). The actual term appears for the first time in Acts after the story of the encounter between the Ethiopian eunuch and Philip. Acts 9:2 states that Saul received authorization from the High Priest to violently pursue men and women of *The Way* and extradite them to Jerusalem (see 24:14, 22; cf. 22:4). Since only the Hellenists were scattered after the

21. Salazar, "Humanizing Pedagogy," 140.

stoning of Stephen in Chapter 7, *The Way* probably designates only the dispersed Hellenist believers and their diaspora converts (after his call on the Damascus Road, Paul joins them as an apostle) (8:1–3; 9:2).[22]

In Corinth where Paul had been speaking in the synagogue for three months, some resisted him and began speaking badly about *The Way,* prompting Paul to move to the public lecture hall of Tyrannus (19:8–10). In Ephesus, a significant civil disturbance broke out initiated by a local silversmith named Demetrius over the impact of the Paul's preaching on the local economy. Apparently, a significant number of Ephesians were forsaking the cult of the local goddess the Great Artemis and joining *The Way* after hearing Paul convincingly teach that gods made with human hands are not really gods (19:21–28; cf. 7:48; 17:24–25). *The Way* seems to be distinct from and yet dependent upon and subordinate to those members of the Jesus movement headquartered in Jerusalem. *The Way* is marginalized in that its disciples and/or apostles are subordinated to the Twelve and the Jerusalem Council (Chapter 15); the Hellenists are doubly marginalized. Also its primary apostles are commissioned from Antioch (13:1–3) or have been exiled from Jerusalem and Rome due to persecution. The believers that accept the good news about Jesus Christ, are baptized and/or are sometimes anointed by the Holy Spirit in response to the proclamation of the diaspora preachers and/or apostles and become members of *The Way.*

One way of knowing or the passive dissemination of knowledge that regards some as more legitimate teachers than others and that requires the indoctrination of the subordinate others in the epistemology and pedagogy of the dominant group does not encourage critical consciousness and mutuality. Knowledge that drives from other than legitimate authority figures, is deficient knowledge and is exposed as such. A hegemonic epistemology perpetuates inequity, injustice, and oppression. "As educators develop consciousness of their own role in upholding inequitable structures, they come to act as oppositional intellectuals who engage critically with authority to develop pedagogical principles that link learning, social responsibility, and political agency."[23] As Cannon asserts, "liberation ethics is something

22. Wilson, *The Gentiles and the Gentile Mission,* 144–45, 150–51, contends that if we accept the position that only the Hellenists and their leaders left Jerusalem, we must assume that significant problems existed between the Hebrews and Hellenists, aside from the neglect of the widows at chapter 6 that would cause the Jews to persecute only the Hellenists, which the Hebrews remain unmolested and "melted into their Jewish background."

23. Salazar, "Humanizing Pedagogy," 131.

we *do*; epistemology is accepting the findings we come to know; womanist pedagogy is the process by which we bring this kind of knowing about
African-American women into relation with a justice-praxis for members
of our species and the wider environment in which we are situated in order
to resist conditions that thwart life, arriving at new understandings of our
doing, knowing, and being."[24]

Humanizing pedagogy aims to raise both the teacher and the students' consciousness about their own privilege, power, and complicity in
oppression as well as the inequities, injustices, and oppressions in society.
As a teacher, I must be willing to be vulnerable in terms of reflecting upon
and sharing my own complicity and privilege in oppressive systems, as I
develop my own "political clarity." Salazar states that humanizing teachers
who would engage in the co-liberation of others must reflect upon their
own history and participation in oppression; they must develop their own
"political clarity"; the goal is a mutual vulnerability.[25] I attempt to model
hermeneutical humility. And I encourage my students to also permit themselves to be vulnerable in the face of their interpretations and those truths
we call absolute, but perhaps are not. I share some of my past and more recent missteps with my students. For example, I have shared how I accepted
certain truths as the only way to understand the Scriptures, as the only way
to know, to be and live in relation to God based on truths (interpretations
handed to me) that I accepted as absolute truths; that I acted in ways that I
am now ashamed of in the name of absolute truth and with the authority of
church office. As a local elder, I tried to persuade a single mother that had
recently escaped from an abusive husband and was trying to make a living
for her young son to reject a job that required her to work on the Sabbath.
I am glad that young African American mother put the needs of her family
first and refused to acquiesce to what I, at that time, believed to be the only
way to know and to be in relation to God and the church.

When assimilation to an elite dominant white male way of knowing
and pedagogy masquerades as a more accurate, universal, standardized,
and decontextualized one-size-fits-all Truth and Faith, the oppressed and
minoritized can be co-opted unwittingly. Salazar asserts that, "Systemic approaches to assimilation are often masked in the language of measurement
and quantification that is rampant in the twenty-first-century educational
discourse. The focus on measurement and quantification in U.S. public

24. Cannon, *Katie's Canon*, 141.
25. Salazar, "Humanizing Pedagogy," 135.

schools results in pedagogical practices that favor high-stakes test-taking skills; foster memorization and conformity; promote reductionistic, decontextualized, and fragmented curriculum; advance mechanistic approaches that are disconnected from students' needs; and reinforce one-size-fits-all scripted practices."[26] In biblical studies courses in general, especially introductory courses, the standard measure to which students are expected to measure up is in their ability to do malestream exegesis as the only legitimate means of explicating a text. In my institution, an exegetical paper is one of the required artifacts used for juried review or assessment as to whether we are teaching and students are learning well. Exegesis is a controlled method supposedly free of eisegesis because students are expected to compartmentalize their examination or discussion of that which is behind the text, in the text, and in front of the text. My students always have a difficult time separating the three, always inserting themselves into spaces that I have been trained to keep them out of. As Salazar notes, "a superficial and uncritical focus on methods often privileges whitestream approaches aimed at assimilation, ultimately robbing students of their culture, language, history, and values, thus denying students' humanity."[27] Constrained by the expectations of my department of which I am a minority, in terms of my gender and race, I eventually decided to reduce weight given to the exegesis paper in the overall course grade. I ask students to begin their exegesis papers with a discussion of their own contextualized identity and how that identity may inform the selection of the text and the reading of the text. I also ask that students devote a page or more to an informed contemporary contextual application based on their reading of the text. But this in my view still reinforces an artificial split between the act of interpretation and the interpreter and her context and concerns. But a "humanizing pedagogy builds on the socio-cultural realities of students' lives."[28] However, scholars of color who struggle to engender a humanizing pedagogy do so within institutions that, "often perpetuate cultural replacement and assimilation into mainstream values and practices through a focus on high-stakes testing, English-only programming, whitestream curriculum, uncritical pedagogy, and deficit perspectives of parents and families."[29]

26. Ibid., 124.
27. Ibid.
28. Ibid., 128.
29. Ibid., 131.

The social context of my students matters. It is also my context too. In my courses, we talk about social injustices, our privilege, our complicity, and our agency, for example, regarding the Flint water crisis (for which we collected money, bottled water, cleansing wipes, and other items); the Detroit water shut offs; the broken foster care system; the rampant sexism in our churches; and the Trump Administration's immigration ban and its impact on immigrants, their families, and on those charged to carry out the ban, including one of my student's family members that works in border patrol and a student who is an immigrant. A humanizing pedagogy is "grounded in the diversity of everyday life and interrogate[s] the human experience in the context of power, privilege, and oppression to provoke action toward humanization and liberation."[30]

What would it mean for a wealthy Ethiopian treasurer from a country where the anointed leader is a black female to join *The Way*, which believed in a Jewish man of the peasant class as God's anointed Messiah? What would it mean for a man who is perhaps physically blemished because of physical castration to accept a Messiah figure whose religion would relegate him to the margins and to become part of a structure that would consign him to marginal space and outsider status? Persons of color should not have to abandon the treasures of their language and culture for a seat in the classroom and to be viewed as persons with little valuable contribution to the learning experience. But students of color are asked in various ways to do just that. María del Carmen Salazar asserts that similar to her own experience "students of color have been compelled for generations to divest themselves of their linguistic, cultural, and familial resources to succeed in U.S. public [and private] schools."[31]

DIALECTICS: THE WAY, THE TRUTH, AND THE FAITH

One way to prevent dialogue is to assert and teach a closed and static notion of truth and to peremptorily teach students to anticipate resistance to the truth and to demonize those who challenge that truth. Patricia Hill Collins writes that, "epistemologically, the act of proclaiming truth speaks

30. Ibid., 142.
31. Ibid., 121.

to the significance of dialogue in constructing truth, especially dialogue across substantial differences in power."[32]

In Acts, the truth is constructed and affirmed based on the decontextualization and recontextualization of the Scriptures. The apostles seamlessly link the sacred tradition with the present events around Jesus, creating good news as the truth. However, the actual words that Philip and Prisca and Aquila speak to the Ethiopian and the Alexandrian Apollos are not revealed. Both the Twelve and other apostles (primarily Peter and Paul) preach the gospel by making connections between the present (the death and resurrection of Jesus or events associated with it) using the demonstrative pronoun "this" and the past or tradition marked by a prophet and/or writings of a prophet and finally linked with the future. For example, in Peter's model speech in chapter 2, he begins with "let it be known to you" (2:14; also at 4:10; 13:38; cf. 15:17) and proceeds to connect the scene at Pentecost in which the various ethnic groups hear the mighty acts of God proclaimed in their different languages with words from the prophet Joel, which has implications for the future. Peter continues by connecting Jesus' resurrection (God raised Jesus) with Scriptures attributed to David and then with the present activity of the Apostles as witnesses. Ultimately, Peter circles back and connects David's words with the spectacle at Pentecost (2:33). Peter does not end his Pentecost speech without connecting the contents of his proclamation with knowing and certainty (*asphalōs*) (2:36). A dialectic is created between the faith and the truth as absolute knowledge. Faith is knowing with certainty in Acts. There is no room for the unknown; even the "unknown god" in the inscription at Athens is made known by Paul (17:22–24). Of course, Acts, like the Gospel of John, states that the only way to experience God's salvation is through Jesus (4:12). Yet, the Hellenists champion and teach the truth of *The Way* in which they themselves are subordinated and marginalized, as well as those whom they teach. In Acts *The Way* is predicated on the truth, absolute truth, a way of knowing and knowing more accurately. The truth remains the same in Judea and in the diaspora and is sometimes referred as "the Faith," as the content of the gospel (6:7; 13:8; 14:22–23; 16:5; 24:24).[33] The Faith and faith (as a verb meaning to believe in something) in Acts presupposes a certain way of knowing or knowledge content. Potential believers are asked to believe the words spoken to them, which are presented to them as words of

32. Collins, *Fighting Words*, 238.
33. Fitzmyer, *Acts of the Apostles*, 351–52.

certainty, primarily based on the experience and testimony of the apostles (1:21–22; 9:20; 10:39; 14:22–23). Believers and/or potential believers are expected to accept the testimony of those who proclaim and teach the good news about Jesus as absolute truth or knowledge. Generally, the manner in which Jews and Gentiles are expected to come to knowledge of the truth is through one of the twelve apostles and later through Paul and other apostles commissioned from Pisidian Antioch (chapter 13). The Hellenists are never commissioned to preach the word of God, but they do and they do so as subordinated non-apostles (nor are they included in the Jerusalem Council where the conflict over the mission to the Gentiles and the basis of their inclusion in the movement was determined). In the construction of the truth and *The Way*, the narrative anticipates opposition to the truth and *The Way*, which is demonstrated through the leaders at Jerusalem and *the Jews* in the diaspora.[34] The anticipated opposition is also voiced by disseminators of the truth like Paul (20:30).

According to Paul Glenn, the philosopher Friedrich Nietzsche theorizes that, "epistemology is a moral issue" and thus is a primary site of struggle "between the strong and the weak."[35] Glenn explores epistemology as a political issue and the function of truth as a survival mechanism. A battle ensues between the weak who have a slave morality and the strong who possess a master morality. The weak need absolute truth for clarity, certainty, and constancy. Clarity, certainty, and constancy allow persons to make quick decisions—to act and label things swiftly and with precision and harmony—which is advantageous behavior for long-term survival. Another tactic of the weak to encourage survival is cooperation, which requires a shared understanding and common language or jargon. A certainty or stability about the world gives comfort to the weak.[36] I suspect that the stability that derives from certainty can be an assuredness about the present and future even if such certainty is knowledge of anticipated disorder and opposition. Glenn writes that, "the epistemological system created out of weakness is assumed by most to be simply true."[37] The epistemology of the weak does not have to be true to be useful. An example of useful but flawed views is the construction of binaries whereby the world is divided

---

34. See Smith, *Literary Construction of the Other*.

35. Glenn, "The Politics of Truth," 575.

36. Ibid., 577.

37. Ibid., 578.

into dualities like good and evil[38] or us and them. Binary thinking usually has no basis in reality; to perceive of something or somebody as "simply good or evil is to do violence to reality."[39] Glen states that another component of the epistemology of the weak is an "unconditional faith in truth," which also assists in survival.[40] What happens when "the truth" clashes with reality and threatens the very survival of "the weak" and the protections it was created to provide?

Conversely, the strong flourish on ambiguity and uncertainty. The epistemology of the weak is used as a weapon against the strong. "Epistemology . . . is a moral undertaking" that is an interested and subjective study of ways of knowing; our interests and objectives shape our epistemologies and signify a group's character. "Our notion of truth is rooted in who we are."[41] And our identities are too often constructed in relation to and over against others—others that we both admire and fear.

WEALTH AND ELOQUENCE AS FETISH/DESIRE AND FEAR/ANXIETY

That which people admire and desire in others is also often feared. Rome wanted to conquer Egypt because of its might, rich culture, and intellectual prowess as much as it desired the wealth and military might of Ethiopia. Gay Byron argues that the Kandake (Queen) of Ethiopia was a major threat to the Romans.[42] The Romans highly valued wealth and eloquence. These two social characteristics are foregrounded in Luke's description of the Ethiopian eunuch and of Apollos, respectively. Luke describes Apollos as a Jewish man who is a native of Alexandria as well as an eloquent man (*anēr logios*) and capable in the Scriptures (18:24); he is an intelligent and powerful orator. As a native Alexandrian, he is also Egyptian from the continent of Africa. Luke characterizes Egyptians as wise and commanding orators. In Stephen's speech before the Council, Moses is described as having been

38. Ibid. Based on Glenn's characterization of Nietzsche's thoughts on epistemology of the weak and the strong, it seems that Nietzsche himself was working in binaries.

39. Ibid.

40. Ibid., 578–79. Glenn asserts that Nietzsche does not deny the existence of truth or that it can be known. Nietzsche "rejects traditional notions of truth," but he does not reject "truth entirely," 580.

41. Ibid., 577.

42. Byron, *Symbolic Blackness*, 34.

taught "all the wisdom of the Egyptians" and as consequently powerful with his words and works (7:22, 35). The wisdom of the Egyptians is praised in the context of Israel's deliverance from Egypt. Luke's representation of Moses contrasts with the depiction of Moses in the Torah where Moses describes himself as a man of poor speech and lacking eloquence (Exod 4:10; 6:12, 30). Egyptians, including Moses and Apollos, are depicted as wise or intelligent in Acts. As a man with a reputation for demonstrated eloquence, Apollos might also have had greater access to royal power throughout the Roman Empire, in his homeland of Alexandria, and beyond. Also Apollos may have been a Roman citizen. Byron states that, "The social and legal status of Egyptians was a point of confusion for many Greco-Roman authors. The citizens of three Greek cities (Alexandria, Ptolemais, and Naukratis) had privileges that distinguished them from the remainder of the Egyptian population. Roman citizenship was not given to an Egyptian unless he or she first held the citizenship of Alexandria. Alexandria, . . . became the political and economic capital of Roman Egypt."[43]

The description of Apollos as eloquent is not fortuitous. Eloquence (*logia*) was a trait or skill highly valued among the Greeks and the Romans; an orator was welcomed in the emperor's palace/house for no other reason than his reputation for eloquence or wealth, even if he otherwise lacked social position or was derided due to some external physical defect. Plutarch writes the following about Publius Clodius a man who had an affair with Caesar's wife Pompeia: "there were no disturbances in consequence of Caesar's praetorship, but an unpleasant incident happened in his family. Publius Clodius was a man of patrician birth, and conspicuous for wealth (*ploutos*) and eloquence (*logos*), but in insolence and effrontery he surpassed all the notorious scoundrels of his time."[44] Similarly, a eunuch that did not have the privilege of wealth and/or access to wealth and position would not have enjoyed the same benefits of status and/or reputation within certain aristocratic circles in the Roman Empire as an Ethiopian eunuch that has authority over all the treasury of the Candace of Ethiopia.

Plutarch also writes that Caesar himself became famous for his eloquence: "At Rome, moreover, Caesar won a great and brilliant popularity by his eloquence (*logos*) as an advocate, and much good will from the common people for the friendliness of his manners in intercourse with them,

43. Ibid., 34.
44. Plutarch, "Life of Caesar," IX.1.

since he was ingratiating beyond his years."[45] Caesar, Plutarch writes, "in his reply to Cicero's 'Cato', he himself deprecated comparison between the diction of a soldier and the eloquence (*logos*) of an orator who was gifted by nature and had plenty of leisure to pursue his studies."[46] In the *Life of Cicero*, Apollonius says to Cicero: "Thee, indeed, O Cicero, I admire and commend; but Greece I pity for her sad fortune, since I see that even the only glories which were left to us culture and eloquence (*logos*), are through thee to belong also to the Romans."[47] Greece could no longer claim a monopoly and superiority over the Romans since they too were known for culture and eloquence as demonstrated in the *Life of Cicero*.

Cicero succeeded in getting a law rejected having won over the tribune when he "overpowered" (*kratethentas*) them by his eloquence (*logos*), for Cicero "beyond all others showed the Romans how great a charm eloquence (*logos*) adds to the right, and that justice is invincible if it is correctly put in words."[48] Tacitus in his "Dialogue on Oratory" discusses the incomparable renown and prestige of those classes of men in Rome who excel in public speaking and he mentions two individuals who excel in eloquence and are known to ends of the earth. Sometimes eloquence is wealth: "I would make bold to affirm that our friend Eprius Marcellus, of whom I have just been speaking, and Vibius Crispus. . . are just as well known *in the uttermost parts of the earth* (in extremis partibus terrarum) as they are at Capua or Vercellae, which are mentioned as the places of their birth. And it is not their great wealth that they have to thank for this—200 millions of sesterces in the one case and 300 in the other—though it would be possible to hold that it is to their eloquence (*eloquentiae*) that they owe that wealth: no, what makes them famous is simply their eloquence. In all ages the divine influence and supernatural power of eloquence have given us many illustrations of the high position to which men have climbed by sheer intellectual capacity."[49] Eloquence is wealth and wealth is eloquence. And both wealth and eloquence can override an objectionable or derisive physical presence in Roman circles and can give one admittance to the Emperor's inner circle: "Though they had sources of wealth, though neither of the two was of pre-eminently high moral character, while one of them had

45. Plutarch, "Life of Caesar," IV.2.
46. Plutarch, "Life of Caesar," II, III.2.
47. Plutarch, "Life of Cicero," III.2.
48. Plutarch, "Life of Cicero," Xii.5-XIII.1.
49. Tacitus, "Dialogue on Oratory," 8.1–3.

an exterior that made him even an object of derision, yet after being now for many years the most powerful men in Rome, and—so long as they cared for such success—leaders of the bar, they take today the leading place in the Emperor's circle of friends, and get their own way in everything."[50]

Eloquence is supernatural power and emanates from a divine presence. Apollos spoke boldly in the synagogue in Ephesus (18:26). Such boldness is associated with the Twelve and Paul who have been anointed with the Spirit (4:13; 9:27). Social mobility can be achieved through eloquence and wealth. Eloquence is a combination of delivery and content. Priscilla and Aquila circumscribed Apollos's content, effectively diminishing or subsuming his eloquence to *The Way*. Similarly, even before the Ethiopian eunuch requested baptism as a sign of his submission to or acceptance of *The Way*, his invitation to Philip to join him in chariot might also be understood as symbolic of conquest. In his first-century poem, *De Rerum Natura* (*On the Nature of Things*), Roman poet and philosopher Lucretius (c. 99 BCE—c. 55 BCE) climbs into the chariot of the muses having conquered his enemy.[51] Lucretius' epic poem uses military imagery that depicts the poem's arguments as a battle over the reader's mind. Perhaps, the battle for the Ethiopian eunuch's mind was won when he invited Philip to join him in his chariot in order to help him to understand the meaning of the text from Isaiah.

Rome finally conquered Egypt in 30 BCE, expanding its boundaries toward the "ends of the earth." Ethiopia, however, was another matter. Ethiopia was always a threat to Rome. Luke wants his readers to recognize the Ethiopian eunuch's social status, regardless of his possible physical deficiencies, as stated above. As Aaron Perry argues, the Ethiopian eunuch's identity is a more complex intersectional identity that embodies both power and disadvantage,[52] neither necessarily canceling out the other.[53] Luke's

50. Ibid., 8.3.

51. Lucretius, *De Rerum Natura*, 6.47.

52. Perry, "Lift up the Lowly and Bring Down the Exalted," 52. Perry argues that the Ethiopian eunuch should be understood as an "Ethiopian-eunuch-official-worshiper." While "eunuch" is a dominant identifying characteristic appearing four times (vv. 34, 36, 37, 38) in the narrative, it is important to remember that eunuchs had political power that "is ideal for political rule," 59. Kartzow and Moxnes ("Complex Identities," 184–204) have also attempted to hermeneutically demonstrate the complexity of the eunuch's character using the theoretical approach of intersectionality.

53. Scholars who argue that the eunuch is a castrated man and that his physical deficiency overrides all other characterizations of him in Luke's narrative include Conzelmann, *Acts*, 68; Johnson, *Acts*, 155; Kartzow and Moxnes, ("Complex Identities," 198–99)

eunuch is no ordinary eunuch. As a non-Jewish man, he owns a copy of the Isaiah scroll and is able to read it, rides in a chariot, holds a position in the court of the Queen of Ethiopia, has responsibility for all of her treasury, and travels distances in the service of the Queen. Skinner argues that the Ethiopian eunuch, although representative of the "'other' or someone who dwells on the 'edges,'" must have some "independent wealth and intercontinental connections" since he possesses a scroll of Isaiah.[54] Abraham Smith also writes that, "Luke's authorial audience, having at least a general knowledge of the Septuagint, would have based their view of the Kushites (and other Africans) on the consistent typological portrait of this nation as one to be revered for its wealth, wisdom, and military prowess."[55] According to Smith, the label "eunouchos" could very well designate a military official; that both the eunuch and the centurion, as royal representatives "belongs to a type of figure notoriously cast as one with better access to royal power than the average citizen,"[56] similarly to Apollos as a man of eloquence. Pervo states that the Ethiopian eunuch as a convert "is a great catch, socially and symbolically," and he is both a marginal character and a "male member of the ruling class."[57] He represents Roman desire—wealth and ruling class status—things Rome desires and fears.

By subordinating and subsuming the Ethiopian eunuch and the eloquent Apollos from Alexandria into the Jesus movement, the superiority of Rome is subverted. By constructing these two significant individuals subordinated to *The Way* through subordinated non-apostles, Luke accomplishes their double marginalization. *The Way* becomes a geopolitical power able to compete with Rome in terms of its membership and co-optation of wealth and eloquence, which Rome so highly valued. Just as Shelley Matthews has argued that high standing, noble women are part of the missionary propaganda of Acts, the ethnic other and his eloquence, wealth, and social status can be similarly viewed.[58]

In Acts, both Ethiopia and Egypt are conquered or subordinated synecdochically in the persons of the Ethiopian eunuch and the Alexandrian Apollos. As Richard Pervo asserts, Philip, like Cambyses, Alexander

---

view the eunuch as an "ambiguous 'other.'" Haenchen, *Acts*, remains uncertain, 310.

54. Skinner, *Intrusive God, Disruptive Gospel*, 61.

55. Smith, "Generic Reading Analysis of Acts 8:26–40," 227.

56. Ibid., 227–28.

57. Pervo, *Acts of the Apostles*, 222.

58. Matthews, *First Converts*.

the Great, and Apollonius of Tyana, also "becomes a sort of 'conqueror' of Ethiopia,"[59] something Rome was not able to fully accomplish. And as Kartzow and Moxnes assert, for Luke's readers/hearers, the Ethiopian eunuch "would be associated with a danger to Rome."[60] Aaron Perry argues that by the end of the eunuch's baptism, the text demonstrates a reconsideration of the eunuch's power: the eunuch's chariot as one sign of his power or wealth disappears from the narrative when he dismounts it in order to be baptized on *The Way*. Those markers previously associated with his wealth are no longer mentioned. Thus, Perry argues that God has brought the eunuch down in an ideological act of reversal after his baptism; the exalted are made low as in Mary's *Magnificat* (Luke 1:52a).[61]

Thus, Philip demonstrates success among a significant person of wisdom, who has some wealth and status, and who is in the service of the Queen. The social and geopolitical status of the submissive and converted Ethiopian eunuch demonstrates the power of the Jesus movement to do what Rome has not been able to do. Thus, through Philip's cooperation with the Angel of the Lord and God's Spirit, Ethiopia is synecdochically conquered. And the same is true of Alexandria, the intellectual and cultural center of Egypt, through the ministry of Prisca and Aquila to Apollos. Luke's method of teaching in *The Way* is much like that of the Roman Empire, which prioritizes one-way knowledge and values wealth and eloquence.

Transformative pedagogies do not silence, marginalize, and reinscribe hierarchical form of knowledge production that value some cultures more than others and encourage a bifurcation in readers and in reading practices. Subordinated and minoritized peoples can be easily co-opted into participating in their own subordination and oppression by accepting uncritically a stagnant notion of absolute truth that is falsely blind to cultural context and universal, even though constructed primarily by and from the perspective of whitestream, malestream, and mainstream scholarship. Gloria Joseph states that a black feminist pedagogy with the goal of liberating humankind "is designed to enable students . . . to re-examine and see the world [and texts] through a perspective that would instill a revolutionary, conscious, liberating ideology."[62] Joseph asserts that a "most radical approach to dealing with the problem of radical educational change

59. Pervo, *Acts*, 222.
60. Kartzow and Moxnes, "Complex Identities," 196.
61. Perry, "Lift Up the Lowly and Bring Down the Exalted."
62. Joseph, "Black Feminist Pedagogy," 467.

would be to focus on the blacks, Latinos, native Americans—the domestic third world people—as the vanguard."[63] She reminds us that education has been used to create and maintain a racialized society and it will be central in the struggle to dismantle a racist society.[64]

63. Ibid., 463.
64. Ibid.

CHAPTER FIVE

Slavery, Torture, Systemic Oppression, and Kingdom Rhetoric

An African American Reading of Matthew 25:1–13[1]

O ppressive structures are often adjusted to accommodate the changing fears and desires of the (neo)colonizers and/or dominant oppressors. The public face of an oppressive system can change or alternate, at times, between oppressor and oppressed subordinated other; aspects of the new facade may even appear representative of the oppressed. But the death-dealing policies continue to the detriment of the oppressed. Oppressive systems must be exposed and deconstructed or dismantled (even in sacred texts), not simply recycled or cosmetically adjusted to palliate and opiate the oppressed and their allies. Studies have proven that black women and men, the poor, and other peoples of color are unfairly targeted by law enforcement; that they are more likely and disproportionately the victims of police profiling; that they receive longer prison terms for lesser crimes; that they are stereotyped as lazy, hypersexualized, and capable of more violence and criminal behavior than others; that as a group they make less money than their counterparts for doing the same jobs; and that despite all this they are expected to embrace a politics of respectability (elitist ideology

1. This chapter is reprinted here with permission of Fortress Press as the copyright owner. It originally appeared as Mitzi J. Smith, "Slavery, Torture, Systemic Oppression, and Kingdom Rhetoric: An African American Reading of Matthew 25:1–13," in *Insights from African American Interpretation* (Minneapolis: Fortress, 2017) 77–97.

requiring them to quietly lift themselves up, acquiescing and genuflecting to unjust laws and practices, and resulting in victim blaming), even when justice eludes them and their rights are diminished.[2] Oppressive systems must be named, particularly those structures that are embedded or reinscribed in sacred texts and contexts.

The biblical text sometimes lends itself to the support of oppressive structures in societies. A gospel narrative, inclusive of slave parables replete with stereotypes, did not have to be perverted to support the inhumane system of slavery and its routine physical, spiritual, and psychological cruelties against African slaves. Matthew's Gospel, for example, abounds with slave parables in which exemplary stereotypical slave behavior serves as a model for persons desiring membership in the kingdom of heavens. Missionaries seeking to convert the black "soul" on southern American slave plantations recognized the usefulness of slave parables to help perpetuate slave ideology, making the connection between the "faithful slave" and the divine master. Palmer's *Plain and Easy Catechism* for slaves included the following prayer: "Help me to be faithful to my owner's interest . . . may I never disappoint the trust that is placed in me, nor like the unjust steward, waste my master's goods."[3] Former slave Frederick Douglass recalled how Master Thomas would bind and for hours flog his crippled cousin Henny. After each brutal beating Master Thomas would proclaim the following: "That servant which *knew his lord's will, and prepared not himself,* neither did according to his will, shall be beaten with many stripes"[4] (emphasis mine). It was inexcusable for a slave to be ignorant of and/or fail to meet the master's demands, to be unprepared to fulfill his subordinate status as slave. If it was determined that a slave was negligent, most masters showed little mercy.

Unjust systems wreak havoc on the lives of the marginalized and the poor and make it possible to condone and justify their victimization. In the slave parables, slave ideology and brutality are reinscribed, sanitized, and sanctified with theological rhetoric. In Matthew 25:1–13 and its immediate context, the master/slave relationship with its stereotypes, fears, and

2. See Alexander, *The New Jim Crow*; Neely, *You're Dead So What?*; Harris and Lieberman, *Beyond Discrimination*; and Douglas, *Stand Your Ground*.

3. Byron, "A Catechism for Their Special Use," 110–11. See Smith, "US Colonial Missions to African Slaves," 57–85. See also Gosse, "Examining the Promulgation and Impact," 33–56; Okyere-Manu, "Colonial Mission and the Great Commission in Africa," 15–32.

4. Douglass, *My Bondage, My Freedom,* 201.

cruelties function as a legitimate metaphorical exemplar for participation in the kingdom of heavens. In this essay I read Matt 25:1–13 through an African-American interpretive lens that prioritizes black people's historical and contemporary experience with oppressive systems. My interpretive lens engages the slave testimony of former African slave Frederick Douglass's autobiography, *My Bondage, My Freedom*, Page DuBois's examination of the etymology of the Greek word *basanos* and its development to refer to state sanctioned testing by torture in ancient texts, Homi Bhabha's postcolonial theory of "ambivalence" and the function of stereotypes, and Ange-Marie Hancock's social political theory of "a politics of disgust" that operated in the Welfare Reform debates. I argue that the ten virgins in the parable are stereotyped slaves, entrapped in an unjust, oppressive structure, who function as the potential collective bride of the bridegroom.

RE-READING THE PARABLE: EXPOSING OPPRESSIVE STRUCTURES

I read the parable of the ten virgins (Matt 25:1–13) in its literary context and as part of a trilogy of slave parables (the other two are about the faithful and wise slave overseer in 24:45–51, and the master's distribution of talents to his slaves in 25:14–30). In the parable of the ten virgins, which is peculiar to Matthew, Jesus likens the kingdom of the heavens to ten virgins (*parthenoi*) that go to meet the bridegroom. All the virgins take their lamps, but five are characterized as foolish (*mōrai*) for their failure to carry contingency oil. The five wise (*phronimos*), having carried additional oil for their lamps, are prepared for the groom's late arrival. The bridegroom delays (*chronizontos*) his appearance so long that all the virgins fall asleep. When all the sleeping virgins are awakened by the midnight alarm of the groom's arrival, the five foolish had burned through their oil. The five wise have oil reserves but seemingly insufficient to share with the five foolish. The wise virgins admonish their foolish sisters to buy their own oil. When the foolish had gone, the groom arrived. The overly-prepared wise virgins arise, light their wicks, and resume as if they had not fallen asleep. With lighted lamps in the dead of night, the wise virgins greet their groom and enter into the final portion of the wedding festivities (*tous gamous*).[5] And the door is closed

5. The use of the plural form of the Greek word *gamos* (wedding) at Matt 25:10 likely indicates that the wedding celebration had several components. The plural *gamos* is also used in Matt 22:1–10 (cf. Luke 14:16–24), which is the story of the king who gave a

behind them. When the five foolish virgins return requesting entrance, the master (*kurios*) rejects them: "I do not know you," (25:11, 12. At v.13). The moral of the parable is given: "Stay awake, therefore, because you know neither the day nor the hour [of the master's arrival]."[6]

This parable, together with the slave parables that frame it, reinscribe oppressive structures, stereotypes, and tactics, including torture, particularly in the form of sleep deprivation. Tortured submissive slaves are presented as exemplary participants/members of the eschatological kingdom of the heavens, and God is likened to a harsh slave master. When God is represented as a patriarchal slave master in Scripture, many readers are reluctant and/or will not permit themselves to critique the harmful stereotypes and unjust systemic demands inscribed in the text, or the oppressive depictions of God. Further I propose that the kingdom rhetoric itself is very problematic.

ABSENTEE BRIDE OR SLAVE BRIDES?

Most interpreters have resigned themselves to the conclusion that the bride is absent from Matthew's wedding parable in chapter 25.[7] Amy-Jill Levine asserts that the ten virgins are "more likely, servants waiting for the groom to return to his home."[8] I propose that the ten virgins are all potential or intended brides of the one groom, and not euphemistically speaking servants, but slave brides. Several ancient interpreters from the early third century through the early fifth century CE arrived at this same hermeneutical position: the virgins are brides. Hippolytus of Rome (170–235 CE) in an allegorical interpretation of the ten virgins in Matt 25 wrote the following: ". . . come, ye maidens, who desired my bride-chamber, and loved no other bridegroom than me, who by your testimony and habit of life were wedded to me, the immortal and incorruptible Bridegroom . . . come all, inherit the kingdom prepared for you from the foundation of the world."[9] Methodius also known as Euboulios, Bishop of Olympus and Patara in Lycia (260–312 CE), in his only complete extant work titled, *Banquet of the Ten Virgins* (or *Concerning Chastity*) praises the virginal life, in both men and women.

---

wedding celebration (*gamous*) for his son and dispatched invitations by way of his slaves.

6. All scripture translations are mine unless otherwise noted.

7. For example, Levine, "Gospel of Matthew," 376.

8. Ibid., 476.

9. Hippolytus of Rome, "Appendix to his works," 252–53.

He too produced an allegorical interpretation of the Matthean parable of the ten virgins, writing that those who preserve their virginity are "being brought as a bride to the son of God." The number ten is symbolic of those who believe in Jesus Christ and have taken the "only right way to heaven." Five also here refers to five senses or "pathways of virtue—sight, taste, smell, touch, and hearing." Methodius further states that those who have maintained their virginity are "all under the one name of His spouse; for the spouse must be betrothed to the Bridegroom."[10] Finally, St. Augustine of Hippo (354–430 CE) also read the parable allegorically. Similar to Methodius he understood the five and five (ten virgins) as representative of five senses. Augustine asserted that the wise virgins represent those having good works in the catholic church of God. Together the five represent the church, or the bride, that is espoused to "one husband."[11]

I imagine that the virgins had completed their nuptials and were journeying to the groom's residence to consummate the marriage, the final stage of the ceremonies.[12] Significantly, the Greek word *gamos* (*wedding*) appears only late in the parable when the groom arrives and enters into the *gamos* with "the prepared women"/wise virgins (25:10). Also the parable as extended metaphor need not signify a contemporary first-century CE social practice or ideal, but it could reference knowledge of a shared cultural past. When Rome and other ancient slave societies (and some not considered slave societies, like Israel) conquered other nations, they often enslaved the most useful human plunder. Some situations resulted in the taking of female virgins, forcing them to become wives to their captors. For example, in Judg 21:12–23, the tribes of Israel conquered Jabesh-Gilead and enslaved 400 young virgins, giving them to the Benjaminites as wives. When additional virgins were needed, Israel plundered virgins from Shiloh. According to legend Romulus (Rome's first king) and his men, seeking an alliance with Sabine, took at least thirty Sabine virgins as wives.[13] Among the most important uses for slaves were sexual and marital functions.[14] I propose that the social practice or ideal the parable references is the wedding festivities

10. Methodius, *Banquet of the Ten Virgins*, 331.

11. St. Augustine, *The Works of St. Augustin*, 402.

12. Everitt, *Cicero: The Life and Times of Rome's Greatest*. When Cicero married in 79 BCE, after the wedding ceremony, the bride journeyed to her bridal home to meet her new husband and to consummate the marriage; preceded by a little girl carrying a torch. This elaborate ceremony was generally eliminated after the late Republic.

13. Plutarch, "Life of Romulus," 29–31.

14. Patterson, *Slavery and Social Death*, 173.

of virginal female slaves, forming a Matthean slave trilogy; it is sandwiched between two other slave parables. The female slaves were given to a king or some other powerful figure as potential brides/wives; this fits well with the emphasis on kingdom. The king was the ultimate master; he could take as many wives as he pleased, when he pleased. Contrary to Jennifer Gancy, Luke 12:42–48 is not the only parable to mention female slaves.[15]

In the trilogy of slave parables, Matthew's Jesus reads master/slave relations through the lens of a divine or sacralized kingdom rhetoric. Sacralized kingdom rhetoric sanitizes and obscures the oppressive power dynamics inherent in the master-slave ideology signified in the parable. The cruel master-slave relationship is idealized and presented as exemplary. And depictions of stereotypical master-slave relations become foundational and a component of iconic kingdom rhetoric creating an unholy alliance.

FEAR, FETISH, AND STEREOTYPES: PUTATIVE TRUTHS AND AMBIVALENCE

Virginity as a social construct carries its own stereotypes (e.g., virgins are modest, prudes, absolutely submissive, girlish, and morally superior). The social construction of women as virgins is grounded in male fear and desire, or what Homi Bhabha calls phobia and fetish. In the labeling of some virgins as "foolish" and others as "wise," the fear/phobia and desire/fetish dichotomy emerges. Masters and oppressive systems desire wise virgins, but wise in their unwavering submission to the system, regardless of circumstance. Foolish virgins are feared because the system cannot control them. Their presence is a threat to the system and the authority of their masters. Bhabha argues that, "there is both a structural and functional justification for reading the racial stereotype of colonial discourse in terms of fetishism. . . . The fetish or stereotype gives access to an 'identity' which is predicated as much on mastery and pleasure as it is on anxiety and defence, [sic] for it is a form of multiple and contradictory belief in its recognition of difference and disavowal of it."[16] Female slaves in the parable of the ten virgins reflect the stereotype that conceives slaves as inherently lazy, evil, worthless and foolish (unless compelled to act other*wisely*). Such stereotypical behaviors are confirmed when half of the virgins fail to conform to the system/master's expectations, regardless of how capricious and unjust. Simultaneously

15. Glancy, *Slavery in the Early Church*, 111.
16. Bhabha, "The Other Question," 106, 107.

and somewhat contradictorily, when slaves do not conform to the system's expectations it is because they are considered naturally inferior. People are either innately slaves or masters, as Aristotle argued. Good and wise slaves are loyal, industrious, useful, and constantly and consciously available or *awake*. An embedded social structure built upon these stereotypes transverses the trilogy of slave parables. Oppressive systems and structures employ stereotypes.

Yet, as Bhabha also asserts, it is insufficient to focus on negative or positive images; we must shift to the *"processes of subjectification"* that stereotypes make possible.[17] We should consider how the stereotype effectively functions. The stereotype functions through *ambivalence,* by stating what is supposedly fact and putative truth *and* also by demonstrating the need to anxiously repeat what is supposedly already known and needing no proof. The stereotype as the major discursive strategy of the discourse of colonialism "is a form of knowledge and identification that vacillates between what is always 'in place,' already known, and something that must be anxiously repeated . . . as if the essential duplicity of the Asiatic or the bestial sexual license of the African that needs no proof, can never really, in discourse, be proved."[18] This process of *ambivalence* is central to the stereotype. I argue that the placement of the three slave parables together in Matthew accomplishes a repetition and a reification of the stereotype across the parables. The stereotypical characterization of the wise and foolish virginal slave women stands in continuity with the stereotypical slaves characterized in the other two parables in the trilogy.

The trilogy (ten virginal female slaves; the faithful [*pistos*] and wise [*phronimos*] slave overseer; and the slaves entrusted with their master's money) illustrates Jesus' admonishment to "stay awake" (*grēgoreō*), which is necessary because of the uncertainty of the Parousia (future coming of the Son of Man), 24:36–44. This same warning summarizes the second parable's meaning (25:13). Several themes found in the Matthean Jesus' instruction about the Parousia are repeated in the slave trilogy: lack of knowledge about the Parousia, the unexpected arrival, marriage, careless and wasteful behavior, watchfulness, staying awake, ownership, and preparedness. Also we notice a focus on division and duality: half are taken/received or commended (the good/wise/prepared/working/awake) and half are left, reprimanded or disposed of (the wicked/foolish/unprepared/idle/sleeping).

17. Ibid., 95.
18. Ibid.

In the parable of the ten virgins, the wise virgins are expected to be prepared for the bridegroom's arrival with constantly burning lamps in order to consummate the marriage. Similarly in the parable of the wise overseer, when the master arrives, he should discover the slave working. In that parable, time is also an issue. In the master's absence the wise overseer is expected to give the master's other slaves their food allowance at the proper time (*en kairō*). The master's delay should not disrupt the expectations that masters have of their slaves and slaves of their masters: A good slave always behaves as if the master sees and knows everything. Conversely, the wicked overseer wastes time in eating and drinking; and behaving like a cruel slave master, he abuses his fellow slaves (24:48–49). Stereotypically, a slave will behave like a master and become the abuser when afforded the opportunity. When the slave overseer shifts from abused to abuser in the master's absence, he is depicted as conforming "to the cultural expectation of ancient audiences."[19]

Knowing that all slaves are potentially "wicked" or "good," the master will arrive at an unexpected time to catch them off guard (24:50). Masters can pronounce slaves as either good or wicked, oscillating between the two, depending on their willingness and ability to respond to the master's every (and ever-changing) whim. The wicked slave will be mutilated and cast among the hypocrites where there will be "weeping and gnashing of teeth" (24:51). "No slave society took the position that the slave, being a thing, would not be held responsible for his actions,"[20] or failure to act.

In the third parable in the trilogy, similar to the parable of the wise overseer, the soon to be absent master entrusts his slaves with his property (25:14–30). The master's property consists of all he owns, including the slave's body/sexuality, time, labor, and peculium.[21] The master gives each slave a specific amount of money/talents. Each slave increases the master's money except he who received one talent. That slave confesses that his master is harsh and engages in unsavory business practices. Thus, acting from fear, he chooses to bury the one talent, rather than risk losing it and suffering the cruel consequences. The master left no instructions that each slave should increase his money; that was an unspoken expectation between

---

19. Harrill, "The Psychology of Slaves," 73.

20. Patterson, *Slavery and Social Death*, 196.

21. Peculium was property and assets that masters placed at the slave's disposal, such as cash, land, clothing or other slaves. Slaves could not own property; the peculium legally belonged to the master. Rodger, "Peculium," 110.

master and slave. Slaves are expected to always fear their masters. But that fear should compel them always to act to further the master's economic interests. The slave with one talent was expected to do exactly what the master would have done: reap where he did not plant. After much time the master returns and rewards the two slaves who increased his holdings with greater responsibilities (more work and less rest!). The slaves that met or exceeded the master's expectations continue in the master/slave relationship. But the wicked, lazy and worthless slave is punished. Like, the wicked slave overseer in the first parable (24:49–50), this wicked slave will also be cast into outer darkness, 25:30. The "wicked" slaves are rendered total outcasts (beyond social death) to be forever subject to torture: "there shall be weeping and gnashing of teeth" (Matt 8:12; 22:13; 24:51; 25:30; Luke 13:28). A slave never escapes torture or the stigmatization of her being.

The most prominent dimension of Matthew's representation of slavery is "the slave's body as the locus of abuse."[22] The abuse may be more evident in the case of the first and third slave parables than in the parable of the ten virgins. I propose that the abuse against the slaves' bodies, including the foolish virgins, is also manifested in the expectation (and failure) of the slaves to make their bodies and labor constantly available to the master. The virgins are expected to stay awake until the groom arrives, no matter how long his delay and how tired they may become. And in their fatigue, they are expected to consummate the marriage. Slave bodies should be perpetually available to the groom's/master's desires. The master's capricious refusal to let the five foolish virgins participate in the final festivities constitutes their rejection as wives; virgins are good for nothing if not to become wives.[23] Their rejection is their "weeping and gnashing of teeth" experience. When virgins taken from conquered peoples are rejected, they are subject to further social isolation or physical death—"slavery is the . . . violent domination of naturally alienated and generally dishonored persons."[24] That which saved them from physical death—their virginity—is rejected.

By their failure to overly prepare for the master's/groom's capricious delay, the five foolish virgins fail to manifest in their bodies the truth of their availability to the master's unmitigated desires; it is a failure to bring

22. Glancy, *Slavery in the Early Church*, 113.

23. See Foskett, *A Virgin Conceived*, 44–55.

24. Patterson, *Slavery and Social Death*, 13. Patterson offers a comparative analysis of slavery based on 66 of the 186 slaveholding societies listed by George Murdock's sample of world societies.

the truth into the light, to make it known, recognizable. Masters determine what is knowable, recognizable or legitimate. The neglect exhibited by the five foolish virgins (insufficient oil) maybe understood as "forgetting." The Greek noun *alētheia* (truth) bears some connection with the idea of "something not forgotten, not slipping by unnoticed."[25] Forgetting is to leave knowledge hidden, a failure to uncover truth, to bring it to a point of utility or usefulness.

In summary, the three parables share a stereotypical characterization of slaves and slavery as a system of oppression: Slaves are expected to respond to their master's whims; to demonstrate unwavering loyalty to their masters; to be "wise," but only with regard to fulfilling their slave duties and not foolish in falling short of expectations; to expect cruelty from their masters, especially when they fail to perform; to be dispensable if they do not perform in ways that furthers the master's economic interests and physical desires; and to be concerned only with pleasing the master. Good and wise slaves do not challenge the system or their servitude. The kingdom of heaven is revealed in the loyalty, vigilance, and wakefulness of slaves, but it is also grounded in difference—differences among slaves as well as between slaves and masters.

STAY AWAKE!: SLEEP DEPRIVATION AS TORTURE AND EXTRACTING TRUTH

In contemporary American society we are experiencing an epidemic of police brutality against black and brown bodies. Even the United Nations' Human Rights Council has officially recognized this epidemic of racism and police violence against minorities in the US as a human rights violation.[26] In America, the burden is once against placed on the backs of African Americans and other people of color to avoid violent police interactions by conducting themselves in certain "respectable" ways. Not only are people of color as victims of biased policing and police brutality under assault from outside of their communities, but some elite members of their communities blame them for their victimization for failure to practice "respectability politics." But as history and contemporary events have demonstrated "respectability politics" will not save one's life when systems and structures remain oppressive and unjust. African Americans and other people of color

25. DuBois, *Torture and Truth*, 84, 85.

26. Sheriff, "US Cited for Police Violence."

are to increase their vigilance, taking care to never arouse the suspicion or fears of police officers or neighborhood watch people (primarily white) in the manner of Trayvon Martin or Keith Lamont Scott; both are, of course, dead. African Americans must stay 'woke, always answerable to a "respectability politics" that requires that black people never express an attitude, move too fast, open-carry with a permit in open-carry states, change lanes without signaling, or walk or run away from a police officer, lest they meet an untimely and brutal death at the hands of authority figures for whom the same wakefulness and prudence is not always required.

As the slave parables in biblical texts demonstrate, slaves should never over sleep or fall asleep when they are expected to be awake and working in a way that displays their subordinate status (cf. Mark 13:34–35). The slave body was unable to rest at night.[27] Seneca, on the mistreatment of slaves, states that a slave whose duty it was to serve wine was forced to "dress like a woman" and compelled to "remain awake throughout the night, dividing his time between his master's drunkenness and his lust."[28] Some slaves were ordered to serve food all night "hungry and dumb."[29]

Similarly, African slaves in America were expected to work from sun up to sun down—"the night is shortened on both ends."[30] Frederick Douglass wrote that, "more slaves are whipped for oversleeping than for any other fault."[31] Slaves were not afforded regular beds but were given "one coarse blanket" on which to sleep. However, the greatest problem was not the lack of a proper bed but the "want of time to sleep," since the present day's field work and preparation for the following day's labor consumed most of their sleeping hours leaving little time to care for their own domestic needs like washing and cooking.[32]

Slavery itself and the pervasive cruelty to which slaves were subjected, as stereotypically inscribed in the slave parables, in ancient slave societies and in American slavery, was torture. Similar to how slaves in antiquity were tortured to extract truth from their bodies in disputes between masters, African American slaves were "sometimes whipped into the confession of offenses which [they] never committed"; on plantations slaves are not

27. Glancy, *Slavery in Early Christianity*, 105.

28. Seneca, *Epistulae Morales*, 7, 8.

29. Ibid., 3.

30. Douglass, *My Bondage, My Freedom*, 102.

31. Ibid.

32. Douglass, *Narrative of the Life of Frederick Douglass*, 287.

considered innocent until proven guilty (the same can be said of many African Americans murdered in this twenty-first century by police officers).[33] "The *basanos* [testing by torture] assumes first that the slave always lies, then that torture makes him or her always tell the truth, then that the truth produced through torture will always expose the truth or falsehood of the free man's evidence."[34] Regarding American slavery, Douglass writes that, "[s]uspicion and torture are the approved methods of getting at the truth. . . . It was necessary for me, therefore, *to keep a watch* over my deportment, less the enemy should get the better of me"[35] (emphasis mine). More specifically, sleep deprivation routinely imposed upon slaves or required on particular occasions to meet the master's special needs should also be viewed as torture.

Wise slaves stay awake to serve their masters; good slaves are constantly available to masters. Wicked/foolish slaves fail to stay awake *and* are unprepared to meet the master's needs; they are denied participation and/ or "citizenship" in the kingdom of the heaven. Douglass writes that, "[t]he good slave must be whipped, to be *kept* good, and the bad slave must be whipped, to be *made* good."[36] A society based on slave/master hierarchy requires torture to produce good slaves and control wicked ones. Viewed through the slave parables, the kingdom of the heavens, like the ancient polis, maintains a social hierarchy of slave and free. DuBois asserts that torture in ancient Athenian society, "[i]n the work of the wheel, the rack, and the whip, the torturer carries out the work of the polis; citizen is made distinct from noncitizen, Greek from barbarian, slave from free."[37] DuBois omits sleep deprivation as a form of state sanctioned torture. I propose that sleep deprivation is both integral to torture of any kind and constitutes torture in its own right.

In the slave trilogy a connection is made between wisdom and staying awake/sleep deprivation: wise and faithful slaves will be awake when the master arrives. All slaves entrusted with the master's property and money should have remained vigilant regarding the master's expectations. The ten

33. Ibid., 277.

34. DuBois, *Torture and Truth*, 36. *Basanos* evolves from a literal meaning of "touchstone" to a metaphorized sense of a test and then returns to a concrete meaning of actual physical testing of a slave's body by torture.

35. Douglass, *My Bondage, My Freedom*, 277–78.

36. Ibid., 258–59.

37. DuBois, *Torture and Truth*, 63.

virginal slaves should not have fallen asleep waiting for the master's arrival. The over-preparedness of the five wise virginal slaves saved them, despite the fact that they too fell asleep. They at least gave an appearance of being continually awake and vigilant; they jumped up from their sleep to trim and light their lamps as if their lamps had never gone out. It would have been hazardous to their health had the ten virgins fallen asleep and left their lamps burning. Regardless of the lateness of the hour, the virginal brides were to be prepared to consummate the marriage. Such physical sacrifice made them wise. A slave who continues with her duties despite sleep deprivation—torture—is of superior value, is considered faithful and can enter into the master's bridal chamber and be known by him. Manifested in the wise submissive slave's body is the truth of the master's total domination over her.

The effective extracting of "truthful" testimony through torture relies on the consciousness of the slave. A slave must be awake for torture to be operative. Inherent to all torture is sleep deprivation—a sleeping slave is not, cannot be, a tortured slave; he cannot feel pain and give testimony to truths when sleeping. A truth that is inscribed in the slave's body daily is the truth of his inferiority and the master's superiority. How is the "truth" of the slave's inferiority inscribed in his body and then extracted? Truth is both inscribed and extracted from the slave's body by his submissive obedience, especially in the master's absence, and through acts of torture, i.e., sleep deprivation, beatings, crucifixion/lynching, withholding of food, and dangling before her promises of liberties that free-born persons enjoy. The Matthean slave trilogy uses staying awake as a test of loyal slaves who in their submission embody truth about the kingdom of the heavens; it demands wakefulness. Sleep deprivation and other forms of mundane cruelties like whipping constituted the American slave plantation as judicial space where slavery and slaves were always on trial. The slave's body daily endures systematic torture/punishment as a sort of truth-telling.

The ancients did not seem to make a distinction between torture and punishment when it came to slaves,[38] but in certain spaces torture or punishment of slaves was communally authorized and codified for the purpose of settling disputes between masters requiring slave testimony. The ability of slaves to function satisfactorily despite and because of abuse (e.g., sleep

38. For example, on p. 55 of DuBois's *Torture and Truth* she inserts a quote of the last speech from Antiphon's First Tetralogy (ii, d, 7), which partially reads "whereas this slave, who gave us no opportunity of either cross-examining or torturing him—when can he be punished? No, when can he be cross-examined"? Also see p. 38.

deprivation) served as a testimony to the slave's suitability for slavery. Du-Bois asserts that, "the slave, incapable of reasoning, can only produce truth under coercion, can produce only truth under coercion. . . . Proof, and therefore, truth, are constituted by the Greeks as best found in the evidence derived from torture. Truth, *alêtheia*, comes from elsewhere, from another place, from the place of the other."[39]

To torture a slave as a witness is a means of extracting truth from a body deemed otherwise unable or unwilling to proffer truth. There is only distortion or absence of truth when slaves fail to meet the system's demands and the master's expectations. Slaves that carry in their sleep-deprived bodies the truth of their subordination are considered wise. Wisdom is associated with truthfulness in the biblical text.[40] Five of the virgins were wise because they rendered the necessary and ostensibly uninterrupted service to the groom/master despite falling asleep.

WISDOM AND A GENDERED APARTHEID

Kimberly Russaw argues that, "prevailing scholarly treatments of Wisdom Literature rarely ascribe wisdom to female characters. Wisdom is personified as feminine in Proverbs, but biblical scholars rarely argue for women as the beneficiaries of wisdom and [such] scholarly treatments of wisdom are overwhelmingly male-centered."[41] Even the wisdom of the ten virgins, is androcentric; they are wise in relation to the slave master/groom's expectations. "Like the slave body that needs the supplement of the *basanos* [testing of the body through torture] to produce truth, the female body and the fragmentary text are both constructed as lacking."[42] Both lack the capacity for loyalty and truth until they demonstrate loyalty and truth, how and when the master demands. The five wise virgins show their wisdom by anticipating and adjusting their behavior to meet the demands of an unjust playing field, which compels them to be over prepared and less than generous toward their sisters. According to Russaw a wise woman is skillful and crafty, possesses the ability to see things (not necessarily in foretelling the future), and pursues what she understands to be good.[43] The five wise

---

39. Ibid., 68.

40. Deutsch, "Wisdom in Matthew," 17.

41. Russaw, "Wisdom in the Garden," 226. See Fiorenza, *Jesus Miriam's Child*.

42. DuBois, *Slavery and Torture*, 95.

43. Russaw, "Wisdom in the Garden," 227–29.

virgins demonstrate skill and craftiness (cf. 10:16) and servile foresight in expecting the master's delay.

The only other wise female in Matthew is Lady Wisdom (*hē sophia*) justified by her deeds (11:19; cf. 11:25, 23:34; Luke 7:35), but who is masculinized in the person of Jesus who "assumes Wisdoms' roles,"[44] especially by the performance of powerful deeds (11:19–20). Matthew redacts his sources to show that Jesus is not "primus inter pares [first among equals] among Wisdom's messengers, but rather to be identified with personified Wisdom itself."[45] The five wise virgins remain the only women in Matthew labeled as wise. But their wisdom is not *sophia* wisdom, but *phronimos* or intelligence circumscribed and mollified by their status as enslaved virgins. Not even the Virgin Mary is described as wise in Matthew (cf. Luke 1:48, the Virgin Mary is a lowly slave [*doulē*]. Yet, the male child that she births is "filled with wisdom" [*sophia*], Luke 2:40). Slaves are not innately good or wise (*sophos*), but they are wise (*phronimos)* in relation to other slaves, reinforcing the stereotype of the slave as inherently foolish, lazy, and/or wicked.[46] Truth/wisdom must be extracted from slaves; they need masters who torture them. In the Synoptics, the Greek noun *phronimos* occurs only in parables or parabolic sayings and "applies to those who have grasped the eschatological position" of human beings.[47] Thus, in the slave parables, the word is applied to those slaves who accept and demonstrate their subordination, which transcends the eschatological Parousia. In God's eschatological judgment, slaves remain slaves.

Just as some slaves are considered wicked/lazy or faithful/wise, the rhetorical division of women as wise and foolish can be viewed as a gendered apartheid. Matthew favors this division. The Q material at Matt 7:24–25 is the parable of the wise (*phronimos*) and foolish (*mōros*) men who build houses on rock and sand, respectively (Luke's version does not characterize the men as wise or foolish, 6:47–49). The man who builds his house on the sand is wise in relation to another man and with respect to building a house with the proper foundation. Similarly, as I have shown, the wise virgins are wise in relation to other virgins and with respect to being presciently prepared for the groom's late arrival. The wise virgins are not the same as the Prov 31 woman who is described as wise *and* virtuous. Slave

---

44. Levine, "Gospel of Matthew," 472.

45. Deutsch, "Wisdom in Matthew," 35.

46. See Garnsey, *Ideas of Slavery from Aristotle to Augustine*, 74.

47. Betram, "*phronimos*," *TDNT* 9:234.

women can be virgins but not virtuous. The Prov 31 woman is an elite, free woman of means. She owns slaves, providing food for her household and duties for her slave girls. She can buy fields and hardly ever goes out at night; she can afford to give to the poor and needy. But the five wise virgins cannot afford to share with their sisters in their hour of need; all are slaves and therefore not encouraged to act communally within a system of apartheid. Dividing people within oppressed groups, giving them a false sense of superiority over their sisters and brothers, is characteristic of racial and gender oppression. If oppressors can convince the oppressed that the noncompliant behavior of their brothers and sisters to systemic oppression is the cause of their suffering, then the system itself is rendered innocuous and truthful.

If the broader public and policy makers can be convinced of the truth-fulness of a negative stereotype, creating a disgust for those who are stereo-typed, then the stereotype becomes effective. Thus, readers automatically accept the designation of five virgins as foolish condoning their fate and ultimate rejection. Ange-Marie Hancock says that a "politics of disgust" preserves the hegemony of the stereotype, creating/maintaining a context of inequality by silencing the voices of the oppressed and destroying any political solidarity between elite classes and the oppressed. Such was the case in the 1996 policy debates around welfare reform that resulted in biased and unjust policies based on the myth of the welfare queen. Elite sisters of all races abandoned poor black women whom President Reagan dubbed, and falsely so, the face of the so-called welfare queens. Micro-level personal or individual explanations are employed to the exclusion of systemic explanations.[48] As Emilie Townes notes the welfare queen con-struct is a modern version of the black matriarch; they fail to model "good" gender conduct, refusing to be passive, which "leads to the stigmatization of Black women who insist on controlling their sexuality and fertility."[49] Further, as Townes argues, such stigmatized black women "do not serve the interests of the classist, racist, and sexist social order of the fantastic hegemonic imagination."[50] The "fantastic hegemonic imagination traffics in peoples' lives that are caricatured or pillaged so that the imagination that creates the fantastic can control the world in its own image."[51] Each parable

48. Hancock, *Politics of Disgust*, 25.

49. Townes, *Womanist Ethics*, 117.

50. Ibid.

51. Ibid., 21.

in the trilogy reinscribes master-slave caricatures through which the author hopes to promote and/or discourage certain behaviors. Certain submissive behaviors are promoted as worthy of participation in the kingdom; such behaviors encourage and reward individualism and classism within an oppressive system that serves as a vision for kingdom relations. Slaves who stay awake at all costs, submitting to the extraction of the truth of their subordination from their bodies, exemplify those who can participate in the kingdom of the heavens. In the parables slave master ideology constructs and controls the kingdom of the heavens.

SLAVERY AND KINGDOM RHETORIC

Like Luke's Gospel, Matthew contains more slave parables than Mark or John.[52] The Matthean Jesus' use of parables comparing the kingdom of the heavens to the stereotypical interactions between masters and slaves is tantamount to conforming the gospel and the character of God/Jesus to the master/slave paradigm, rather than transforming relationships and oppressive systems into the likeness of a loving, compassionate God. By systematically framing slave parables in kingdom of the heavens language, the author of Matthew mollifies the cruelty of slavery, sanctifies the language that signifies the oppression and makes it difficult for (neo)colonized, oppressed and/or marginalized "people of the book" to fully name, reject, and heal from oppression and oppressive systems. What might have been the psychological and social impact of these slave parables and their kingdom rhetoric on first-century believers, many of whom might have been slaves themselves? The Jesus movement appealed to slave and free, master and slave, noble persons and peasants.[53] The social reality of systemic oppression signified by slave parables, baptized in kingdom of the heavens rhetoric, promotes stereotypical slave behavior and oppressive relationships as ideals worthy of imitation and transcending time and space. Also such parables, including the parable of the ten virginal slave brides, reinscribe stereotypes that justify the subordination of certain peoples and systems of hierarchical oppression.

52. According to Glancy, *Slavery in the Early Church*, 107, "[no] trajectory of the Jesus tradition lacks slave sayings."

53. Patterson asserts that "It is generally accepted that Christianity found many of its earliest converts among the slave populations of the Roman Empire, although the fact is surprisingly difficult to authenticate," *Slavery and Social Death*, 70.

Further, our trilogy of slave parables, and similar parables used to teach about the nature of the kingdom of the heavens/God and its participants, continue to reinforce the long-standing marriage of kingdom building, slavery, and religion/theologies. Slavery is a function of nation and empire building and maintenance; historically empires conquer and enslave. Slavery is an inherent and putative aspect of kingdom/nation building providing a reservoir of free human labor compelled to work day and night. This fact raises the question of the appropriateness of "kingdom" language as a metaphor or descriptor for a justice- and love-oriented community. According to 1 Sam 8:10–18, God warned Israel against replicating kingdom building because their sons would be conscripted, their land, labor, and slaves confiscated, and the people would become slaves of the king. Slavery is understood to be a putative reality of kingdom building/maintenance. But it is preferable to own slaves than to become a slave; to be the victor rather than the victim, the oppressor and not the oppressed. When oppressive structures are not dismantled but are occupied by even good-meaning folks and replicated, some *will be* oppressors and others *will be* oppressed.

Matthew inundates his readers with kingdom imagery and language. In the genealogy, Jesus is the Messiah through the Davidic royal dynasty (1:1, 16–18, 20). As one of the most famous and beloved kings in Israelite history, David's dynasty would be perpetual, so said the Deuteronomistic writers (2 Sam 2:7). In Jesus the kingdom of the heavens had come near. John the Baptist, Jesus and his disciples preached the good news of the kingdom of the heavens (3:2; 4:17; 10:7). In Matthew alone, Jesus is called the "king of the Jews" toward the beginning of the Gospel in the same narrative context that introduces King Herod (2:1). Herod, the puppet king and extension of the Roman Empire, fears that the baby Jesus is the rumored "king of the Jews" who might grow up to usurp his place. The kingdom rhetoric and the significant and numerous presentations of servile slave behavior and good master/slave relations as exemplars demonstrate that Matthew is not a "counternarrative" or "work of resistance," as Warren Carter once argued. Nor does Matthew position himself or speak against the status quo of Roman hegemonic imperial power,[54] at least not consistently or without contradictions. Matthew does not seek to change the system, just the face of those occupying positions of authority within the system. Filling the same old oppressive structures with different people

54. Carter, *Matthew and the Margins*, 1.

is deceptive; a new driver does not a new car make. Carter has argued that reading and hearing Matthew as counternarrative "unveils and resists a center that comprises the powerful political and religious elite."[55] More recently Carter concluded that Matthew both critiques and imitates Roman imperial practices and ideas;[56] Fernando Segovia states that Carter reads Matthew as a "conflicted text."[57] Matthew as conflicted text may be a more accurate characterization. It seems that Matthew too often, particularly with his use of slave parables, speaks from and stands in the center of the status quo. The colonized sometimes unwittingly internalize their own oppression. As Musa Dube argues, the Matthean community is not subversive to Roman imperialism; Matthew is a postcolonial text, written by the subjugated, that certifies imperialism,[58] if unwittingly. I wonder whether Matthew could have been a slaveholder like Philemon. Perhaps Matthew was a wealthy slaveholder who was as prosperous as the "relatively wealthy urban community" reflected in his Gospel.[59] Or maybe Matthew was neither a slaveholder nor a wealthy person, but simply a victim of colonization who unintentionally co-opted his own oppression by inscribing slavery and kingdom of the heavens rhetoric in his text. Readers accept the union of kingdom rhetoric and slavery as holy and sanctified because it is inscribed in their sacred and authoritative text. "What God has joined together [religion, slavery/oppression and kingdom building] let no human being separate" (Mark 9:10).

Few kingdoms have been built without the use of slave labor. The fact that the method for the theological teaching is a parable, an extended metaphor, does not mitigate the oppressive nature of the social phenomena and ideals that the metaphor makes use of. "A memorable metaphor has the power to bring two separate domains into cognitive and emotional relation by using language directly appropriate to the one as a lens for seeing the other."[60] As an expanded metaphor, the parable like all metaphors allow us to visualize what is otherwise abstract.[61] Géza Kállay asks whether

55. Ibid., 3.

56. Carter, "The Gospel of Matthew," 99–100.

57. Segovia, "Introduction," 32, 52. See also, Segovia, "Postcolonial Criticism and the Gospel of Matthew," 221–28.

58. Dube, *Postcolonial Feminist Interpretation of the Bible*, 133.

59. Boring, *Gospel of Matthew*, 104.

60. Black, *Metaphors*, 236.

61. Kállay, "Some Philosophical Problems about Metaphor," 339.

a metaphor conveys some (heuristic) "knowledge" or is it "just ornamental
. . . how is it related to the being of the human being?"[62] As an expanded
metaphor, the parable is discourse. Discourse conveys knowledge. Simi-
les (for example—"the Kingdom of God is like") are a type of metaphor,
a discourse comparing one thing to another, conveying knowledge. It is
similarity created in the act of connecting a metaphor with a subject.[63]
There are some sentences or narratives that employ metaphors that we
might determine to be plainly false.[64] Metaphor is the means to dismantle
the dead, thingly, categorical, fixed character of objects, ideas, and concepts
by making them do something, by almost forcing them to perform actions.
Metaphor does not only describe reality, it also creates it, it animates it.
And by showing the alien in terms of the familiar through something relat-
able, metaphor may give us the impression of familiarity and/or call our
attention to unfamiliarity through some—familiar—indirect connection.
Metaphor is seeing (something) as; it brings us into proximity with things
which, for example in their abstraction, seem to be distant. Metaphor is
thus able to tell us how we are in the world. [65] *And I would add how we ought
to be in the world.* Thibodeau and Boroditsky argue that metaphors suggest
commonality and likeness. A metaphor's power is covert. "Unbeknownst
to us, metaphors powerfully shape how we reason about social issues."[66]
Studying the connection between metaphors used to describe crime and
solutions to crime (based on the findings of five research experiments),
Thibodeau and Boroditsky "found that metaphors exert an influence over
people's reasoning by instantiating frame-consistent knowledge structures,
and inviting structurally-consistent inferences . . . people chose information that was likely to confirm and elaborate the bias suggested by the metaphor—an effect that persisted even when people were presented with a full
set of possible solutions." Further, the authors state that metaphors supplied
their participants with "a structured framework for understanding crime
. . . influenced the inferences that they made about the crime problem,
and suggested different causal interventions for solving the problem," even
when the metaphors themselves were not particularly influential.[67]

62. Ibid., 339.
63. Ibid., 340, 342.
64. Ibid., 343.
65. Ibid., 345.
66. Thibodeau and Boroditsky, "Metaphors We Think With," 9.
67. Ibid., 9.

King and kingdom gradually became appropriate metaphors for God and God's governance despite the Scripture's depiction of God rejecting kingdom or nation building as the antithesis of theocracy—rule by God alone. Is rule by God alone ever possible among human beings? This transition was preferred despite the oppressive manner in which kings/kingdoms have behaved historically.[68] Perhaps only one kingdom in history has been built without the use of enslaved labor. The Gentile Persian King, Cyrus the Great (and his successors), liberated the Jews from Babylonian captivity and built his kingdom using skilled paid laborers, refusing to use slaves. Cyrus is the only Gentile to be named God's Messiah; he was known to be a just man and others tried to follow in his steps. But typically, slavery is an integral aspect of kingdom building. Most of the kings of Israel and Judah are described as doing what was evil in the sight of God. And even when they are described as doing good, it is within the framework of the politics of kingdom maintenance.

By systematically creating a metaphorical relationship between slave-master relations and the kingdom of the heavens and God, Matthew contributes to a normalizing of the violence inherent in the enslavement of human beings, sanctifies the language that signifies the oppression, and makes it difficult for (neo)colonized, oppressed, and/or marginalized "people of the book" to fully name, reject, and heal from oppression and oppressive systems. The cruel existence of the tortured slave that the metaphors rely upon is precisely useful to help the audience visualize what the kingdom expects of its subjects. The parable of the ten virgins is a slave parable and is part of a trilogy. In the trilogy the trustworthy tortured slave and the harsh master is touted as an ideal to be imitated by those wishing to participate in the kingdom of the heavens. The expectation of preparedness predicated on being in a constant state of wakefulness or sleep deprivation is a form of torture integral to slave life, and to contemporary black life in America. Through the tortured enslaved body the truth of her subordination and the master's superiority was daily extracted. On such tortured bodies, kingdoms, colonies, churches, and universities have been built.[69] I propose that the iconic kingdom rhetoric should be rejected. Should our theology be ground in such cruelty and barbarism? DuBois writes that a "principal motive of [political] torture . . . is control, the domination of an unpalatable truth. That truth may be communism, nationalism, democ-

68. See Hanson, *A Political History of the Bible in America.*
69. See Wilder, *Ebony and Ivy.*

racy, any number of threatening political beliefs that disrupt the unity, the unblemished purity and wholeness of the state, or of any entity analogous to the unitary philosophical subject."[70] That, "unpalatable truth" may also be egalitarianism or justice, which threatens the privilege of those who benefit from the injustice of racism, sexism, classism, heterosexism, and other isms in society at large, in our churches or in our educational and theological institutions.

As noted, God is not depicted as a different kind of king than the ones that ruled over Judah and Israel. Linking God's kingdom with David's dynasty carries a normalizing tendency toward dynasty, greed, and materialism, gender violence, violence against the other, and war. In kingdoms, the paradigmatic representation of patriarchalism and kyriarchalism, conquered and colonized foreigners are not safe but are enslaved, slaughtered, or otherwise abused, and their women and children raped or murdered. Kingdoms and nation-states must protect their borders from outside others, and maintain a hierarchy among inside others and "freeborn" citizens. As previously stated, when the Israelite people decided they wanted a king like all the other nations, it was articulated as a rejection of God, particularly because of the violence that such a political entity would inflict in order to establish and maintain itself; violence is a normal aspect of kingdom building and maintenance.

Matthew's Gospel depicts Jesus as the Davidic Messiah King like no other canonical Gospel. Even in the birth narratives, readers are encouraged to excuse or overlook the impact of violence, as collateral damage and to adopt a means-to-a-end viewpoint. I wonder if the inclusion of certain Gentile women in the genealogy invites readers to excuse or justify the violence committed against them or their communities: It is conceivable that Ruth, the Moabitess, was forced to become Naomi's daughter-in-law by virtue of being a prize of war—a virgin sold to the winners as wife-by-rape and later encouraged to seduce Naomi's distant relative so that Naomi might have an heir. Yolanda Norton observes that Ruth must assimilate and turn her back on her people and this is often ignored; the characters in the book of Ruth, more often than not failed to show her genuine hospitality.[71] Rahab turned on her own community to save herself; and Bathsheba was coerced by power and authority to submit to rape by King David, who subsequently orchestrated the death of her husband to hide the truth of her

70. DuBois, *Slavery and Torture*, 149.
71. Norton, "Silenced Struggles for Survival," 266–80.

pregnancy by David. Perhaps the foreigners who are accepted as outsiders within are those who accept their own oppression and that of the others in their communities. Every nation draws a line between insiders, outsiders, and dangerous outsiders within its borders. It is usually, of course, the wealthy foreign immigrants within a nation's borders who are often given a pass. For religion to align itself with nation building and maintenance, it must normalize certain kinds of violence committed against the constructed other; and women or children are the most vulnerable as objects of violence. But to speak a life-giving, hopeful, living word from God, our sacred texts "cannot be read simply as authoritative or normative visions of life as it should be."[72]

Herod the King is a violent man, and despite being a puppet or client King of the Roman Empire, having no autonomous nation to rule over, serving a colonized people, he will and is able to inflict violence to protect his throne and power. The baby Jesus escapes Herod's attempt to murder the King of the Jews, but many babies do not. Many mothers who could not cross the border into Egypt because of poverty or detainment watched their children being slaughtered. Is the reader invited to stop and mourn them? Could not God protect God's Messiah son *and* the other children as well? If Jesus is indeed the King of Jews, is he to assume Herod's place. If so, he too would be under the thumb of a foreign power expected to uphold the same oppressive structures. And Matthew, reinscribing what Mark had written, depicts Jesus as stating that a person can both satisfy the Emperor's demands and the demands of God, as if the two never conflict. To acquiesce to the Emperor's power is necessarily to limit the power of God on earth for justice and peace.

Matthew 25:31–46 has been a favorite teaching of mine as it seems to demonstrate Matthew's interest in social justice. However, I now believe that it places more emphasis on acts of social justice (feeding the hungry, visiting the sick and imprisoned) than on actually changing those systems that promote the perpetual existence of poverty, hunger, prison nations and enslavement, and sickness, as opposed to equity, health, wholeness, protections, and freedom for all. Acts of social justice are necessary and good where inequity and poverty abound, to help keep people alive and healthly in the meantime. But systemic change is necessary to destroy poverty, inequities, and injustice. I don't believe we love a God who encourages the normalization of violence. God is emotionally vulnerable toward love and

72. Tolbert, "Reading for Liberation," 270.

justice.[73] And the more we feel what God feels, the more we too will become emotionally vulnerable toward love and justice and develop an aversion for violence. Martin Luther King Jr. once wrote, "The aftermath of nonviolence is the creation of the beloved community, while the aftermath of violence is tragic bitterness."[74]

73. Sirvent, *Embracing Vulnerability,* 68.
74. King, *Stride Toward Freedom,* 102.

CHAPTER SIX

Moral Authority, Insignificant Young Bodies, and Sacralized Violence

Reading 2 Kings 2:23–25 through the Lens of Police Brutality

The Christian church in the USA is a segregated institution. This racial divide came into sharp relief during the 2016 presidential election when approximately 80 percent of white Christian Evangelical Protestants (and about 60 percent white Catholics) supported and voted for Donald Trump as President.[1] Among whites in general, 58 percent voted for Trump. Conversely, he received only about 8 percent of the African American vote; 88 percent overwhelmingly voted for Hillary Clinton.[2] Evangelical Jerry Falwell Jr., President of Liberty University, christened Donald Trump as the dream President for Evangelicals.[3] The racial divide in the Christian church is indicative of a racialized America, which is painfully apparent in other areas of American life. White and nonwhite Americans are divided on the issue of policing and police brutality in the USA. The murders of young

1. Bailey, "White Evangelicals Voted Overwhelmingly for Donald Trump"; Stewart, "Eighty-one Percent of White Evangelicals Voted for Donald Trump."

2 Durkee, "Here's the Breakdown of How African-Americans Voted in the 2016 Election."

3. Mazza, "Jerry Falwell, Jr. Calls Donald Trump 'the Dream President' for Evangelicals."

African American males and females like 7-year-old Aiyana Stanley-Jones in Detroit (2010), 17-year-old Trayvon Martin in Sanford, Florida (2012), 22-year-old Rekia Boyd in Chicago (2012), 16-year-old Darnisha Harris in Breaux Bridge, Louisiana (2012), 23-year-old Shantel Davis in New York (2012), 18-year-old Michael Brown in Ferguson, Missouri (2014), 12-year-old Tamir Rice in Cleveland, Ohio (2015), and 15-year-old Jordan Edwards in Balch Springs, Texas, and too many others, rocked communities of color and ignited the Black Lives Matter Movement (the BLMM). Despite the fact that many of the deadly encounters were captured by cell phone cameras and body cameras, primarily majority white juries have refused to find police officers (and a community watch person) that violently took black and brown lives guilty. And too often a simple defense that the officer or civilian feared for his or her life, regardless of whether the victim had a gun or other deadly weapon, was running away, or had committed no crime, is sufficient for such juries to deliver a not-guilty verdict. In the case of the May 2017 murder of Jordan Edwards by a police officer in Balch Springs, Texas, the officer who shot Edwards was surprisingly quickly fired and arrested a few days after the incident. Whether justice will prevail in the courts is another matter. Many people of color would agree with Kelly Macias who wrote in the *Daily Kos* that, "If you're a white, 15-year-old honor student, chances are you won't get shot and killed by police officers with rifles."[4] The failure of America's justice system to hold police officers that commit these crimes accountable leaves a gaping wound in communities of color.

The majority of white Americans perceive that instances of police brutality can be attributed to a few rotten apples in the barrel (it is an individual problem), while others, primarily people of color, argue that the barrel is rotten (it is an institutional or systemic problem).[5] Racism regards all people of nonwhite races as inferior and less human; the whole barrel is rotten with a few exceptions. In the story of Elisha's encounter with a group of young boys/men readers are given the impression that the entire young crowd is rotten (2 Kings 2:23–25). The prophet Elisha, the successor to the Prophet Elijah, is on his way to Bethel when he encounters the young boys/men who tease and ridicule him. Consequently, Elisha curses them, which presumably results in the appearance of a sloth of female bears that attack and maul the boys. Elijah proceeds on his way. Elisha meets words with

4. Macias, "15-year-old Unarmed Honor Student Shot and Killed Leaving House Party by Rifle-wielding Cop."

5. Weitzer and Tuch, *Race and Policing in America*, 53.

words, but Elisha's words carry the moral force of negatively altering, if not taking, the lives of the young boys/men.

In this chapter, I read 2 Kgs 2:23–25 through a hermeneutical lens that privileges the experiences and perspectives of communities of color, of minoritized peoples, with regard to the epidemic of police brutality. Communities of color perceive of and experience real abuses of power and authority that result in the "televised" murder of the children of women and men of color, with impunity. I address the issue of police brutality in terms of unmitigated, unbridled, and uncritical power and authority. I draw upon Ronald Weitzer and Steven Tuch's work in *Race and Policing in America*. Weitzer and Tuch surveyed Americans' perceptions about race and policing. Their analysis of the survey is informed by the "group-position thesis" and the "power-threat thesis" in the area of race relations and criminology. According to the two interrelated theses, "the interests of the dominant group include proprietary claims to scarce resources," and any challenges to those resources may be perceived to threaten the established racial order.[6] Majority group "attitudes toward other racial groups are therefore positional: shaped by a sense of superiority over minority groups and a need to defend the dominant group against threats to its interests."[7] Conversely, the subordinate group is compelled by experiences and perceptions of biased, inequitable, and exclusionary practices and policies by the dominant group, and by "an interest in securing a greater share of advantages."[8] However, it is not necessarily the advantages that communities of color need when it comes to police brutality; they need to have their rights protected. It is their rights that are being violated; it is more than a matter of advantages or privileges.[9]

What happens when some communities and readers place their trust in authority figures, most of whom are male and perceive them to be above reproach in the performance of their civil (or religious) duties? Most people expect police officers (and ministers of the gospel) to be exceptional role models of morality and good character, to be beyond reproach. This expectation often collides with the experiences and perspectives of people of color, especially African Americans. When the experience of communities of color is different from the dominant majority and the justice system is

6. Ibid., 8.

7. Ibid.

8. Ibid.

9. Zack, *White Privilege and Black Rights*.

represented by and functions from the perspective of the dominant culture, minoritized lives are sacrificed in order to uphold and protect the perspective of the dominant group or the majority perspective. David Marcus argues that the story also demonstrates that disrespect toward the prophets, particularly by the powerful, will not be tolerated and will bring swift retribution from YHWH as it did in the case of the forty-two boys.[10] Inscribed in the bodies of young males is a lesson for those who are perceived as a threat to the dominant group.

When race is a factor in the preservation of the dominant group, even or especially the children of the minoritized group are feared and can be sacrificed with impunity. Historically, black children and children of color have been expected to act deferentially toward white male authority figures (and their women and children) regardless of how the former might (mis)treat the latter. Black children and children of color are expected to demonstrate unmitigated respect and rigid compliance; sass or talk-back and/or physical resistance or retaliation or any behaviors that can be perceived by the dominant culture as disrespect toward authority could result in racial profiling, harassment, arrest, and lynching/death. Any perceived disrespect for sacred and sacralized hierarchal authority figures could and has been met with torture, sexual violence, and murder. Children of color in America have always been expected to shoulder the greater burden of demonstrating unmitigated respect for certain authority figures through unambiguous behaviors of deference and/or a politics of respectability. Inequitable burdens placed on children of color become heavier as behavior that constitutes disrespect and is threatening can change at will, depending on the agenda of the individual authority figure or the practice and disposition of police departments and/or grand juries. Respectability politics is a moving target for communities of color. Thus, "the reality of violence includes its virtual (and not only actualized) presence . . . its potential to both disrupt the ordinary and became part of the ordinary."[11] What remains constant is the will and power of the dominant culture to diminish and/or disregard the rights of children and adults of color based on respectability politics. People of color know that respectability politics is no insurance policy against abusive police officers and their complicit and

10. Marcus, *From Balaam to Jonah*. Elisha is characterized as a prophet who should not be trifled with, particularly by the Omride dynasty. Marcus argues that the story is one of three examples of anti-prophetic satire containing direct or indirect attack on the prophet and unbelievable elements that dominate the story.

11. Das, "Violence, Gender, and Subjectivity," 295.

silence partners, regardless of the race of the latter. The death of Philando Castile and the exoneration of Minnesota police officer Jeronimo Yanez in the courts of law offer a prime example.[12]

Respectability politics and fear of the other is a perennial defense for any police officer who wittingly or unwittingly tramples on the rights of children of color even when, and especially when, the result is murder. Sacred dominant group ideologies about white male authority and respectability politics framed as disrespect, threat, and fear collide to the detriment of communities of color. This essay first examines the socio-historical context of the intergroup conflict between the northern and southern kingdoms in the struggle for dominance, identity, group advantage, power, and moral authority as it relates to place and space. Second, I discuss the significance of young male bodies as sites of struggle within this intergroup conflict. Third, I address the construction and criminalization of the "insignificant" young males as a threat to Elisha as a member of the dominant group. Fourth, the swift retribution that Elisha conjures through a curse against the young males is examined. Finally, I discuss the normalization of violence in the text.

DOMINANT-GROUP AND POWER-THREAT THEORY: KINGS, PROPHETS, AND YOUNG MALES

In the fields of criminology and race relations, group-position and power-threat theories state that racial attitudes reflect "intergroup competition and conflict over material rewards, power, and status in a multiracial society."[13] In the group-position paradigm, prejudice is grounded in a shared "sense of group position" and shared interests of the group drive "underlying contentious intergroup relations and racial attitudes." The dominant group claims exclusive access to scarce resources, challenges to such entitlements may be understood as a threat to the predominant racial (political, religious, or social) order. The dominant group understands itself in terms of a positionality; the dominant group occupies a superior position within society over against the minority group as inferior. The dominant group must defend its interests against any perceived encroachments on or threats by the minority group that challenge the position and claims of the dominant group. Conversely, the subordinated group is motivated by a perception of "unfair

12. Ellis and Kirkos, "Officer who Shot Philando Castile Found Guilty."

13. Weitzer and Tuch, *Race and Policing in America*, 8.

and exclusionary treatment" by the dominant group and "by an interest in securing a greater share of advantages," and their rights protected. Racial attitudes reflect relationships between groups and not just the feelings and beliefs of individuals within those groups.[14]

The context of Elisha's encounter with the forty-two males and their consequent mauling by two she-bears is intergroup conflict wherein the dominant group faces challenges to its political right to rule and its claim to religious superiority. The story is an organic part of 1–2 Kgs, expressing the author's literary and theological concerns.[15] The histories of the Kings, which delineates the split of the Kingdom of Israel into the northern and southern kingdoms, and the subsequent struggles for dominion and identity and over sacred space and the justice of God, is played out between and among prophets and kings. Abraham Heschel states that, "of paramount importance in the history of Israel was the freedom and independence enjoyed by the prophets, their ability to upbraid the kings and princes for their sins."[16] In fact, the prophets reminded the kings of the limitations of their power and sovereignty; that God remained sovereign over all kingdoms; and that God's justice (*misphat*) would prevail. The prophet's authority was unparalleled. The prophet claimed to be "the voice of supreme authority. He not only rivaled the decisions of the king and the counsel of the priest, he defied and even condemned their words and deeds."[17] Yet, as part of the Deuteronomistic history (DH) (Deut–2 Kgs), 2 Kings is infused with and motivated by a sacred ideology or theology that celebrates and privileges an eternal Davidic royal dynasty.[18]

Two different kinds of power and authority are at war—the power and authority of the prophets and the Kings of Israel and Judah. The Kingdom of Judah, or David's dynasty, was already dubbed the winner; Yahweh promised that David's ancestors would forever occupy the throne of Judah (2 Sam 7). The history of the kingdoms of Israel and Judah is told from the standpoint of the dominant group, the one that outlived the other. The prophets as men and women of God are significant actors in this intergroup conflict; they are the moral force and voice of Yahweh and Yahweh's justice. In contemporary American society police officers "often identify

14. Ibid.
15. Irwin, "The Boys and the Bears," 35.
16. Heschel, *The Prophets*, 612.
17. Ibid., 614.
18. Kirsch, *King David*, 11.

themselves as a moral force, protecting innocent and productive members of the public against those who would brutalize and victimize ordinary decent citizens."[19]

In order to prevent the Kingdom of Israel from reverting to the house of David and the people from giving their loyalties to King Rehoboam of Judah, Jeroboam constructed two sanctuaries to compete with Yahweh's house in Jerusalem, one at Bethel and the other at Dan. At each site Jeroboam placed a golden calf and appointed non-Levite priests from among the people; the people worshipped at both sites. But Jeroboam favored Bethel over Dan; he offered sacrifices at Bethel and attached to it a festival day (1 Kgs 12:25–33). Jeroboam also established a separate priesthood, sanctifying them to serve at Bethel (1 Kgs 13:33–34). Bethel would substitute for the house of Yahweh in Jerusalem and hopefully stop the Israelites from going to Judah and solidify Jeroboam's power as King of the northern Kingdom of Israel (1 Kgs 12:25–33).

Once while Jeroboam was offering sacrifices at Bethel, a man of God from Judah prophesied that the altar would be destroyed (1 Kgs 13:1–3). When an elderly prophet situated at Bethel was informed by his sons that the man of God from Judah had prophesied against Bethel and was returning home from Bethel (1 Kgs 13:9–10), he intercepted the man of God from Judah and deceived him. God had instructed the man of God from Judah to fast from food and water while in Bethel. But when a fellow prophet claimed that he received a contrary word from Yahweh, the man of God from Judah is tricked into disobeying Yahweh (1 Kgs 13: 8–9, 18). Ironically, while the two prophets ate, Yahweh spoke to the prophet of Bethel, who subsequently prophesied against the man of God from Judah because the latter disobeyed Yahweh's instructions to fast and return home another way (1 Kgs 13:20–22). Consequently, the man of God from Judah is attacked and killed by a lion after leaving the prophet of Bethel's house (1 Kgs 13:11–25). Yahweh is dead serious about Bethel as a threat to the sanctuary at Jerusalem. After Jerusalem, Bethel is the most frequently mentioned shrine in the biblical text and primarily as Jerusalem's rival. In its popularity, Bethel "threatens and subverts the ubiquitous political and cultic monopoly, centrality and hegemony of Jerusalem dominant in biblical tradition."[20] Different from Elisha, the man of God from Judah failed to do all in his power to avoid any misunderstanding as to where his loyalties

19. Weitzer and Tuch, *Race and Policing in America*, 46.
20. Gomes, *The Sanctuary of Bethel*, 2.

lie and to protect the dominant group and its sanctuary. Jules Gomes states that, "the choice of Bethel as a central sanctuary for the Northern Kingdom in the wake of Jeroboam's revolt and reform was essentially a conservative and populist nationalistic programme"; it was an attempt to "reclaim the nationalistic identity of the Northern Kingdom as the rightful heir to age-old traditions from the early days of the tribal confederation."[21] In the sanctuary at Bethel, Jeroboam fused iconographic elements from the worship of El and Yahweh. Bethel, as a symbol of the golden calf at Bethel, constituted an effort to consolidate the Israelites and the Canaanites under one motif.[22] The selection of Bethel was a masterful move on Jeroboam's part because it was connected with significant ancient traditions, memories, and persons in the history of Israel, including the patriarchs (Gen 28:10–22; 35:1–20; Amos 7:12–13), the exodus event, festival of Sukkoth, and Canaanite conquest.[23] It seems that when Bethel was active it was sometimes perceived by the Deuteronomic redactors "as a threat to 'pure' Yahwism."[24] Both exilic and post-exilic writers accepted Bethel's central role in forming Israel's national identity, but Bethel must be subordinated to Judah or any hope for absolute unity and a new unified nationalism fades.[25] According to DH, Yahweh chose one place as the place of worship and that place is Jerusalem or Zion (Deut 12: 5–7, 12–13; 1 Kgs 8:14–21, 9:1–4); Bethel was regarded as a high place like other high places that YHWH abhorred (1 Kgs 13:1–3; 2 Kgs 23:15–20).

It is against this background, that Elisha *went up* to Bethel from Jericho (2:23). Earlier Elisha had followed Elijah from Gilgal *down* to Bethel (2:1–2). Joel Burnett argues that we might understand the reference to Elijah going up to Bethel rather than down to Bethel "not as topographically correct but as theological and polemical in nature."[26] Bethel was an important and legitimate and relevant sanctuary and/or high place to which Jacob and other worshippers ascended to offer sacrifices (Gen 35:1; Judg 20:18; 1 Sam 10:3; Hos 4:15). Perhaps Elisha's going up to Bethel implies that he intended to offer a sacrifice on the altar at Bethel, to pay homage to Yahweh, as his ancestor Jacob had done at Bethel. Burnett states that references to

21. Gomes, "Nation and Temple," 220.

22. Ibid., 221.

23. Gomes, "Nationalism and Hindutva," 221–28.

24. Ibid., 226.

25. Ibid., 228.

26. Burnett, "'Going Down' to Bethel," 283.

"going down" to Bethel from Gilgal and other geographical places "calls for considering this directional language in relation to symbolic meaning at work" in 2 Kgs 2:23–24 and in its larger literary context.[27] Since Gilgal in our text can be identified as the famous Gilgal in the Jordan Valley, Burnett asks how could it be stated that Elijah and Elisha descended from Gilgal to Bethel? According to Burnett, both Elijah and Elisha's narratives consist of an up/down structure wherein Elisha's ascending and descending mirror that of Elijah's demonstrating a mirror-like "active correspondence" between the two prophets and Elisha as successor to Elijah.[28]

Perhaps Elisha was nostalgically retracing some of the steps he had taken with his mentor, Elijah, to Jericho and Bethel. On the way, Elisha thought it harmless and fitting to offer a sacrifice at Bethel, but he wanted to do so in a way that did not call attention to himself or to the act. However, some young males in Bethel disrupt Elisha's plans. Mark Mercer argues that the best explanation for the boys chiding of Elisha to go up to Bethel "would be to understand the exhortation to 'go up' as a challenge to Elisha to enter Bethel and worship at the cult site established by Jeroboam."[29] They were "exhorting Elisha . . . to stop and make a religious pilgrimage to the cult site in Bethel."[30] To be able to associate Elisha with the Bethel sanctuary would have boosted its popularity.[31] Gomes argues that 2 Kgs 23:25 "could be read positively"; perhaps Elisha worshipped there, manifested his prophetic powers there, and had disciples living there.[32]

THE BODIES OF YOUNG MALES AS SITES OF STRUGGLE

Before analyzing the characterization of the young boys that Elisha encounters on his way up to Bethel, I want to examine how the bodies of young males are constructed as sites of struggle, reflecting and embodying the conflict between the two kingdoms at the level of king and prophet.

27. Ibid.," 286. Additionally, "the topographically incorrect detail of 'going down to Bethel' may be not only an aspersion cast at Bethel but also part of the narrative's avoidance of any implication that Elijah and Elisha worshiped there."

28. Ibid., 288–92.

29. Mercer, "Elisha's Unbearable Curse," 175.

30. Ibid., 176.

31. Gomes, The Sanctuary of Bethel, 57.

32. Ibid.

Young males are used and/or sacrificed as kings and prophets choose and demonstrate their loyalty or disloyalty to one kingdom and its sanctuary over another. The bodies of young males constitute the flesh and blood battlegrounds on which intergroup conflict for domination, identity and moral force is waged. Young males can be and are drawn into the intergroup battles. Sometimes the age of the males is ambiguous, as perhaps in our text. Nevertheless, when one group is feared and viewed as a threat to another group's domination, resources, moral force, authority, and/or identity, all males belonging to the opposing group, regardless of age, pose a threat and are viewed as men, and consequently men are sometimes derogatorily described as young boys.

For example, King Rehoboam of Judah (King Solomon's son) privileged the counsel of "the young boys" (*hayəladim*) he had grown up with over the advice of the elders; the young men advised Rehoboam to deny the people's request that he lighten the heavy labor and discipline that his father had placed upon their backs. Rehoboam took the young men's advice to increase their labor and to discipline them more harshly. These actions lead to a final separation between Judah and the rest of the Israelites. (1 Kgs 12:6–19). This political move draws the anonymous young males into the conflict and they share in the responsibility for Rehoboam's fateful decision.[33] Choon-Leong Seow argues that the young boys are Rehoboam's peers; they are about forty years old. However, they are "derogatorily called 'the boys.'"[34] Yet "the boys" do not pay a fatal price because they are on the side of the winners or the dominant group. However, on the other side of the struggle for domination, identity, resources, and preservation is Jeroboam, King of Israel. Children or youth on the side of the losers, don't fare so well. According to the DH, Jeroboam's son Abijah became ill and died because of the sins of his father Jeroboam. Abijah's death constitutes the fulfillment of Yahweh's promise to "cut off the house of Jeroboam" (1 Kgs 14:14–16). Jeroboam instructs his wife to disguise herself and inquire of the prophet Ahijah about the ultimate fate of their child. It was the prophet Ahijah who had prophesied that Jeroboam would be king over Israel (1 Kgs 11:29–35). Although the old prophet's sight was dimming, Yahweh revealed to Ahijah that it was Jeroboam's wife who visited him and was asking about the child

33. De Vries (*1 Kings,* 156) calls the *yeladim* (young men) "newcomers" and the elders he calls "veterans." He argues that the narrative is written by a "Judahite and loyal supporter of the house of David" and is a "prejudgment" on the king's choice of counselors, 156, 157.

34. Seow, "I Kings," 102.

(1 Kgs 14:2–5). The prophet tells the child's mother that although Yahweh made Jeroboam king over Israel, Jeroboam failed to live up to the moral standard of King David (14:8–9)! Consequently, every male, slave and free, would die. And her son, Abijah, despite that he himself pleased Yahweh, would be the first to die; he would be dead by the time the child's mother returned to the city (1 Kgs 14:6–12; cf. 13:33–34).

ELISHA AND YOUNG INSIGNIFICANT MALES

Like the young boys from whom King Rehoboam of Judah took counsel, the young males that Elisha curses are anonymous. But like Jeroboam of Israel's son Abijah, the anonymous young males in/near Bethel who encounter Elisha, the prophet from Judah, shall be fatally wounded, it appears. It is unclear whether the young males of Bethel are small children, adolescents, or young men. Scholars do not agree on the meaning of the Hebrew plural noun and adjective, nə'arim qətannim (v.23), which can be translated variously. Some scholars regard the addition of the adjective as a clear sign that the males are in fact small children and others understand the function of the adjective as simply reinforcing na'ar to mean "young men."[35] One's interpretation of the two words, as well as how the males are constructed in the narrative, will determine how one views the males. Readers will either sympathize with them or not. Mark Mercer interprets nə'arim qətannim as "insignificant youth," rejecting translations that render them as children; they are "adolescents or young adults."[36] While I do not discount the possibility that the nə'arim qətannim are children, I translate the term as "insignificant young males." In rendering the nə'arim qətannim as young adults rather than as children or boys, one might attribute to them greater responsibility and culpability for their behavior and make it easier to justify Elisha's response. A translation of qətannim as "insignificant" might align with an attempt by the narrator to convince readers to see the nə'arim as subordinate, foreign, or marginalized others in relation to Elisha as the prophet from Judah and as Elijah's successor, regardless of whether they are

35. Burnett, "'Going Down' to Bethel," 296.

36. Mercer, "Elisha's Unbearable Curse," 173. Mercer admits that the collocation of na'ar qat qatōn generally indicates a young child (1 Sam 20:35; 1 Kgs 11:17; 2 Kgs 5:14; Isa 11:6), but he points to Solomon's description of himself at a time when he was twenty years old (1 Kgs 3:7) as one example of how we need not translate the phrase as "little children" (172–73).

children or youth by ancient standards. The *nə'arim* might be understood as other because of presumed loyalty to the southern sanctuary of Bethel, their lack of social standing, their youthfulness (as adolescents or young adults) that also implies lack of wisdom and maturity, and their anonymity. The narrative outcome implies that because of and despite their otherness their behavior is threatening, inexcusable, and deserves severe retaliation.

We find the singular form (*na'ar qatōn*) of the Hebrew phrase *nə'arim qətannim* (young insignificant males) elsewhere in Kings where it refers to males that are not small children. In response to Yahweh's offer to give Solomon whatever he wished, Solomon described himself as a *na'ar qatōn*, which can be translated "small child" or "insignificant young male." However, the meaning seems to be the latter; he is a young man lacking experience and wisdom to govern a people or lead a nation (1 Kgs 3:5–9). He asks for wisdom, and Yahweh gives him wisdom and discernment. Solomon's wisdom makes him famous and significant, whereas before he was relatively insignificant. Yahweh's offer to Solomon did not come with strings attached. Prior to Yahweh's offer it is said that Solomon offered sacrifices and offerings at high places, especially at a sanctuary at Gibeon, a principal high place (1 Kgs 3:3–4). However, after Yahweh gifts Solomon wisdom and discernment to govern the people despite his youth, it is said that Yahweh blames Solomon's many foreign wives for his love of other high places. The other is a convenient scapegoat for what ails one and the ultimate threat.

When God raised up Hadad of the royal house of Edom as Solomon's adversary because of Solomon's infidelity, Hadad was an insignificant young male (*na'ar qatōn*) in comparison to Kings Solomon and David (1 Kgs 11:14, 17, 23). Hadad had escaped the slaughter of Edomite males by David's commander Joab; Hadad fled to Egypt with some Edomite slaves belonging to his father where he stayed until David's death (1 Kgs 11:11–22). Hadad was a young insignificant young male when he fled (1 Kgs 11:17). Like Solomon, Hadad was young and inexperienced and consequently lacked wisdom when he fled. Similarly, the young males in Bethel are insignificant in comparison to Elisha, who is a prophet with moral force, authority, experience, maturity, and presumably wisdom.[37] The insignificant young males in Bethel lack authority, experience, maturity, wisdom, and position.

37. Ibid. In the story of Elisha's encounter with the insignificant/young boys the narrator also refers to the latter as simply young boys at 2:24b. Contrary to Mercer, the literary switch to *yəladim* and without an adjective in verse 24b can be attributed to the brevity of the episode; the narrator established a more detailed characterization at the outset.

The apparent relationship of the insignificant young males to Bethel also constitutes them as other and subordinate. As subordinated others, their behavior is egregious and threatening to the identity, power, and authority of the dominant group and their sanctuary, which is Judah and Jerusalem. Elisha represents the dominant group and its sanctuary.

RESPECTABILITY POLITICS: CRIMINALIZATION AND ANNIHILATION OF YOUNG MALES

Respectability politics soothes our consciences when members of the dominant group treat subordinated others with deadly force because of a perceived threat to the former's domination, advantage, identity, and authority. Alicia Wallace states that spoken and unspoken rules exist for the purpose of regulating the behaviors and appearance of people. Such rules are neither relative nor flexible, "but wide-sweeping and stem from colonialism, privilege, and whiteness. It forces conformity, erases culture, and alters the path of a people. Many of us like to think of ourselves as progressive and liberal, but frequently exercise respectability politics for reasons we may not understand which are rooted in racism, sexism, homophobia. . . . Respectability politics . . . hoists us up on our high horses, and takes away our responsibility for the way we treat other people. It puts the burden on the marginalized person to adjust their appearance or behavior to earn respect from the majority."[38]

Respectability politics does not always protect people of color from the danger posed by biased policing. Disparities between white citizens and African American and Latinx citizens about the impact of race on policing and misconduct "are *not simply a matter of opinion*."[39] The existence of bias in policing is "undeniably real"; police may demonstrate bias against individuals and neighborhoods.[40] The number of young black men who have personally experienced being stopped without good reason, verbal abuse, physical abuse, and observed corruption is double that of young black women,[41] but this fact should not be used to minimize or ignore the impact of such violence on black females. Black women are impacted when their

38. Wallace, "Everyday Respectability Politics."
39. Weitzer and Tuch, *Race and Policing in America*, 55–56.
40. Ibid., 32, 34.
41. Ibid., 54.

sons are unjustly violated and murdered and when they themselves are the objects of police brutality and misuse of authority.

Elisha encounters the insignificant young males in their neighborhood, as he is going up to Bethel. Weitzer and Tuch states that, "research based on police records and on systematic observations of officers on the streets" and perspectives of respondents to their survey "indicate that *at the neighborhood level, police misconduct is largely confined to disadvantaged minority communities.*"[42] It is a liability for law-abiding citizens to live in disadvantaged neighborhoods since many police officers view whole neighborhoods as "troublesome or crime-prone and thus treat all residents indiscriminately; this is known as 'ecological contamination.'"[43] Those who live in or near Bethel, who implicitly or explicitly demonstrate a relationship or loyalty to Bethel, as a competing sanctuary to the dominant sanctuary in Jerusalem might be ecologically contaminated.

The insignificant young males that Elisha encounters on his way up to Bethel, tease him with these words: Go up, bald head! Go up bald head! (2 Kgs 2:23). In fact, the qal imperative of the Hebrew verb 'alah could be translated *go up* or *come up*. The boys could have been intimating that Elisha was having a hard time climbing up toward Bethel; that he should go up; or simply calling unwarranted and unwanted attention to Elisha's going up to Bethel. By addressing Elisha using a negative physical descriptor—bald head—the young males are characterized as disrespecting the prophet. It is unclear whether the young males know Elisha is a prophet from Judah. It is clear that whether or not they are aware of Elisha's identity is not important to the storyteller.

Scholars disagree about the full nature of the young males' crime. Some argue that the assault was only verbal. Others claim that the boys physically stoned Elisha,[44] perhaps to justify Elisha's response. Minimally, the boys are depicted as verbally ridiculing Elisha because of his bald head[45] and his apparent destination. Or perhaps the young males deride Elisha's physical appearance only because of where he seems to be going. Mercer argues that it was a mild offense for the boys to insult Elisha for being bald,

42. Ibid., 56.

43. Ibid., 31–32.

44. Lucian of Samosata. See Stade, *The Book of Kings*, 184.

45. Irwin, "The Curious Incident of the Boys and the Bears," 24. Elisha could have shaved his head as an act of mourning over the departure of his mentor Elijah.

but the "exhortation for the prophet to make a pilgrimage to the cult site of Bethel" constituted what was a more serious and intolerable taunt.[46]

Some readers may assume the view "that boys will be boys," but this explanation is seldom offered for males who are insignificant and/or othered. To the dominant group in a society, subordinated children are seldom perceived in the same way as children of the dominant class. "Boys will be boys" does not shield the subordinated other from being treated as a real threat to the power and privileges of the dominant class. Ziolkowski asks, "what does this tale suggest about male children, particularly in their relation to the sacred (as represented by Elisha)?"[47] Or what does this story suggest about insignificant young male children in relation to what the dominant group considers sacred and authoritative?

In 2017 almost sixty-five years after a white mob, with the moral force of the dominant group, lynched (beaten beyond recognition and murdered) a fourteen-year-old black male Emmett Till (1941–1955) with impunity, Till's accuser, a white woman named Carol Bryant (the then twenty-one year old wife of Roy Bryant), publically admitted in a *Vanity Fair* article that she lied.[48] Bryant, who claimed that Till transgressed the boundary of respectability imposed upon black males (regardless of age) with regard to interaction with white people, especially white women, nonchalantly acknowledged that she perjured herself. Carolyn Bryant (Donham) broke her decades-long silence in a new book *The Blood of Emmett Till.* Timothy Tyson, a Duke University senior research scholar, reveals that Bryant, at the age of seventy-two, admitted that she had made up the most damning part of her testimony: "That part's not true," Donham reportedly told Tyson about her claim that Emmett made verbal and physical advances toward her. Conveniently, according to *Vanity Fair*, Donham said that she could not remember the rest of what happened in the store that August evening in 1955. Till's accuser will face no criminal charges. Regardless, the so-called social transgression she lied about, the burden of racialized and gendered respectability politics, should never have been placed on the backs of black children and their parents. Yet, the dominant society (and some people of color lacking critical consciousness) continues to hoist this burden onto the backs of communities of color. The state of New Jersey recently passed a Bill

46. Mercer, "Elisha's Unbearable Curse," 180.

47. Zoilkowski, "The Bad Boys of Bethel," 337.

48. Weller, "How Author Timothy Tyson Found the Woman"; Edwards, "Woman Who Caused Emmitt Till's Death Admits to Lying."

requiring that elementary schools teach children how to interact with the police![49] Black people had rights and continue to have rights that respectability politics obfuscates and denies.

DEHUMANIZATION OF THE OTHER

The anonymity of the insignificant males, their significant numbers, and the negative behavior attributed to them, contributes to their dehumanization. Ziolkowski argues that what scholars have left unaddressed is "the negative image the tale presents of small boys" in general.[50] The collective bodies of insignificant young males are a site of struggle for demonstration of moral force or authority, domination, sacred space, and identity. The prophets of Judah will go to extreme lengths as will the prophets of Israel and the kings of both kingdoms to conserve and maintain identity, power, domination, and sacred space. The anonymity of the boys, and that they are numbered to be at least forty-two, gives the impression of a gang acting in one accord like a mob; where there is a mob, there is the threat of escalating violence. The number forty-two may be significant in the context of this intergroup conflict. Elisha later commissions a young male prophet (*na'ar nabi'*) to anoint Jehu as King of Israel (2 Kgs 9:1–6). And Jehu subsequently slaughters forty-two princes, relatives of King Ahaziah of Judah, at Beth-eked, presumably because he perceived them to be a threat to Israel's dominance (2 Kgs 10:12–14). Prophets and Kings can be responsible for the violence against, and death of groups, of young insignificant males, with impunity, when they constitute a threat to their power and authority.

Different from the princes of Judah, the insignificant young males connected with Bethel are depicted as a gang from a subordinate group. In the literature from the Renaissance to the present, Ziolkowski found a "clear topos finding its paradigm in . . . the Bethel boys motif," demonstrating the pattern of "an adult, almost always male and notorious for a certain eccentricity or unpopular distinction, is gratuitously mocked, stone, or abused in some other manner by a pack of two or more anonymous street urchins."[51] That the boys are identified in the literature as "street urchins" (or a gang) may demonstrate an interpretative literary trajectory demonstrating a class

49. Luger, "New Jersey Passes Bill Requiring Schools to Teach Kids How to Interact with Police."

50. Ziolkowski, "Bad Boys of Bethel," 336.

51. Ibid., 340.

distinction, attributing to boys of a lower social class behaviors that might be expected of boys in general.

Youth and children (and even adults) often succumb to peer pressure—the curse that the prophet pronounced, and concomitant punishment, assumes all the boys were guilty and that the punishment fits the level of guilt; it also ignores the individuality of the boys and their humanness. It is easier to treat humans abusively when the abuse is inflicted because of group affiliation or a collective identity based on negative stereotypes and othering. The cursed and mauled children become an example for adult readers and particularly for the kings who reign over Israel and others that ally themselves with the wrong sanctuary or who might be tempted to disrespect Yahweh's prophets. Also, the prophet robs the parents, mother and father, of the opportunity to correct their children; he robs them of their parental authority.

A ten-year-old African American child that I was raising was suspended from school for one day. I was told by the white male principal who was substituting for the black female principal that day that my child had hit a male classmate; my daughter's classmate told her that she "should go on Snap Chat and kill herself." The substitute principal claimed that my daughter had been warned on two previous occasions about hitting classmates. When I asked why no one informed me of this behavior, he stated that if it had happened in his classroom, he would have called me. Nevertheless, he used his authority to suspend my child for a full day. By not informing me of my child's so-called previous behavior, the school robbed me of the opportunity to correct her behavior before suspending her from school for a full day. Interestingly, in a recent parent-teacher meeting previous to the incident, my daughter's teacher informed me that my child "made good, mature decisions, unlike many of her peers."

The prophet is not a peer of the insignificant young males. At least forty-two young males are depicted as ridiculing one lone, but powerful, prophet. But Elisha is not any prophet; he is the prophet that refused to leave Elijah's side until he inherited a double share of Elijah's spirit or power—and perhaps, his moral force and authority (2:1–13). Although the work of the prophet is not generally low visibility work, it is when Elisha encounters the young males (or at least he hopes to keep his visit under the radar). In the USA, because policing is "'low visibility' work" it is impossible to know what proportion of police stops are unlawful or unjustified and which are proper.[52] Before police started wearing body cameras, dash cams were installed on patrol cars, and the invention of cell phones and social media, policing was largely concealed from the view of citizens and other officers. However, not all police officers wear body cameras, some have removed them during stops, and others have conducted stops out of range of the dash or body camera. Even when a videotaped stop shows questionable behavior by a police officer and compliance by a citizen who is injured or killed by an officer, predominantly white juries have acquitted or found such officers not guilty.

Persons that commit crimes or engage in illicit behaviors are humanized when their stories are told. When addiction to heroine and prescription drugs like opioids became epidemics in white communities, white and other nonblack addicts were humanized through photo essays, media stories, and documentaries.[53] Humanizing stories probe and reveal familial and personal challenges, achievements, and setbacks that impact or motivate negative, destructive, and criminal behaviors. However, in racialized societies, questionable and negative behaviors of the minoritized and/or foreign other are reported by the media (if reported at all) void of any humanizing context.

SWIFT RETRIBUTION: DIVINE AUTHORITY MANIFESTED BY ABUSE AND VIOLENCE

Elisha's response to the behavior of the young insignificant males is swift, emotionless, and disturbing. Elisha turned and looked at the boys before swiftly cursing them in Yahweh's name. The curse apparently results in the fatal mauling of the insignificant young males by two she-bears. Some commentators view Elisha *and* the she-bears as behaving uncharacteristically.[54] Yahweh and Elisha are depicted as somewhat petty, violent, callous, and thin-skinned. Through a curse, Elisha harnesses and unleashes the violent judgment and revenge of Yahweh. Access to the power and authority to curse in Yahweh's name is conjured as quickly as Elisha can speak; it appears unbridled and unchecked. Ziolkowski states that, "the story is prone to offend the sensibility of the modern reader," as repelling and repugnant,

52. Weitzer and Tuch, *Race and Policing in America*, 48.

53. IFL Science, "Humanizing the Heroine Epidemic." See also Nolan and Amico, "How Bad is the Opioid Epidemic."

54. Ziolkowski, "Bad Boys of Bethel," 337. See Hobbs, "2 Kings," 24.

and shocking,[55] but that may not be the case with the average reader. When I asked the students enrolled in my online Engaging Texts and Contexts course to discuss this narrative, most of them justified the curse and mauling because of the disrespect shown the prophet. While some modern scholars may problematize the narrative, too many average readers, lacking conscientization, criminalize the males. Readers who prioritize a so-called literal, prima facie reading of the Bible because of its sacred authority, find it difficult and sometimes impossible to question violence attributed to God or God's anointed servants in the text (or in their own contemporary contexts), to attribute innocence to a person or persons that is characterized as deserving of violence, and to empathize with the constructed other upon whom violence is inflicted.

The gender of the bears adds to the project of dehumanization. The two she-bears symbolically replace the children's mothers and harshly and perhaps fatally discipline the children as if the males themselves are animals. Using she-bears as the instrument of God's retribution lends credence to and emphasizes the severity of the crime and the appropriateness of punishment. The she-bears' "grisly punitive action against the boys reaffirms the authority and dignity both of Elisha as prophet and of the God he represents,"[56] but it has the reverse effect on the boys. Some scholars view Elisha's cursing and the consequently mauling of forty-two insignificant young males as a negative parallel to the blessing of the spring in Jericho (2:19–22), demonstrating that the prophet has both the power to bless and to curse.[57] Seow argues that by juxtaposing the two healing stories, the narrator is showing the "prophet's power to inflict deadly punishment" parallel with his power to avert death (2:19–22) in the immediately preceding episode. The narrator is making a theological point that a sovereign God, through Elisha's ministry, exercises the prerogative to both bless and/or curse.[58] Irwin argues that the story transcends the issue of respect for Yahweh's prophet but "the covenant curse of wild animals that Elisha pronounces . . . is in itself a prophetic warning—a single, localized event that warms the people of Bethel of worse to come if it persists in its

55. Ibid., 333. See also Ziolkowski, *Evil Children in Religion, Literature and Art.*

56. Ziolkowski, "Bad Boys of Bethel," 339.

57. Burnett, "Going Down' to Bethel," 293.

58. Seow, "2 Kings," 178, 179. See also Irwin, "The Curious Incident of the Boys and the Bears," 23–35. Irwin argues that both stories are part of the covenant based on Leviticus 26:22, which includes both a curse and a blessing meant to warn Israel of the consequences of ignoring the prophetic word.

disobedience."[59] Pronouncing covenant curses is routine part of prophetic oracles in prophetic literature.[60] The prophetic office, as a social institution, is imbued with power to bless or curse in response to intergroup (and intragroup) threats.

POWER-THREAT THESIS AND SOCIAL INSTITUTIONS: SANCTUARY AND PROPHETS

Both the sanctuary that locates God within a particular place and space and the office of prophet are social institutions. Weitzer and Tuch extend the group-position theory to address group relations with social institutions, such as the criminal justice system. One of the social resources to which the dominant group believes it is entitled to have greater access is the criminal justice system. "Coercive crime-control practices may, in the aggregate, benefit the dominant group. More specifically, the 'power-threat' thesis holds that the amount of control exercised by the authorities is related to the real or perceived threat posed by minority groups to dominant groups."[61] Police forces are pressured by the dominant group to exercise more control over cities with a high percentage of black populations and in predominantly white areas with higher numbers of blacks than is comfortable for the dominant group. The power-threat thesis highlights how "group interests structure both police practices as well as citizen perceptions of the criminal justice system . . . policing is not simply a response to individuals or to isolated crimes . . . but is also responsive in a more subtle and diffuse way to a city's racial order and the interests of dominant groups."[62] A "mutual affinity" exists between dominant groups and the police, who view themselves as a moral force. This mutuality is markedly noticeable in more racially polarized and less democratic societies. In the United States the white dominant group tends to associate communities of color with crime and violence and support for the police among the dominant group has traditionally been strong and ubiquitous.[63]

Elisha's demonstration of control and authority seems more important than the lives of perceived enemies. Not only do the stories of healing the

59. Irwin, "The Boys and the Bears of Elisha," 28.

60. Ibid., 28–29.

61. Weitzer and Tuch, *Race and Policing in America*, 9.

62. Ibid.

63. Ibid., 10.

Jericho waters and cursing the insignificant young males establish Elisha as Elijah's anointed successor, but they also solidify Elisha's transition from insignificant, unknown prophet to a moral force and a powerful man of God (1 Kgs 19:16).[64] Immediately after Elisha's curse of the young males, readers are told that Jehoram son of Ahab became King over Israel and is described as doing evil and causing Israel to sin (2 Kgs 3:1–3). An entire people are rendered as rotten apples and this likely includes the forty-two insignificant young males that are mauled by two she-bears. Conversely, Elisha's actions are to be taken as justifiable, morally defensible, and condoned by Yahweh.

When children or young people are othered, subordinated, and marginalized, violence perpetrated against them is mitigated and justified by the dominant society regardless of how slight the act they might commit. What matters is that the act is somehow perceived as a challenge to the authority, moral force, and identity of the dominant group. Such children are seen as an extension of the larger subordinated communities to which they belong. There is no margin of error when it comes to children of color and (dis)respect for or being a perceived threat to certain authority figures that represent the dominant society. African American children, especially black males, receive harsher discipline in public schools than do other students.[65] This seems to be the case at the preschool level as well.[66] Within the past few years too many videos have surfaced showing school police officers flipping children out of their seats and throwing them against walls, as occurred, for example, in a South Carolina public school classroom in 2015.[67]

Primarily all-white or nearly all-white juries continue to return not guilty verdicts in cases where primarily white police officers and community watch persons kill the children of the "insignificant" other in the blink of an eye out of fear and because they have the moral force and authority of the majority to do so. The retribution based on perceived threats and fear is swift against "insignificant" black and brown bodies; and justice is slow, rare and nonexistent. This part of the interaction between Elisha and the insignificant young males brings to mind the recent murder of fifteen-year-old African American Jordan Edwards in Texas, and twelve-year old

64. Irwin, "The Boys and the Bears of Elisha," 33, 34, 35. The story also shows that disobedience or obedience to the prophetic word results in either curse or a blessing.

65. Lewis, "Black Students Face More Discipline."

66. Khadaroo, "Racial Gap in Discipline Found in Preschool, US Data Show."

67. Fausset and Southall, "Video Shows Officer Flipping Student in South Carolina."

African American Tamir Rice, and other young black males, who have died as a result of encounters with police officers. Jordan was shot while riding in a car with his friends; Tamir Rice was fatally shot after someone called 911 to report a "guy with a pistol" that was "probably fake." Police arrived to see Tamir alone and within two to three seconds one of the responding police officers shot him dead; the gun was a toy, as the 911 caller had reported.[68] But the officers were acquitted.

The prophet proceeds unmolested. The prophet is very human and very vulnerable, as are the bodies of the subordinated others and their children. But Elisha is easily offended and abusive. How does one tell if a prophet has abused his authority? Who decides if a prophet has abused his authority? Is it the people that are responsible and given the authority to test the prophet? If so, which people—the dominant class? The sacred text because of human bias, out which the text is created, and that is embedded in the text cannot be read uncritically. As Hugh Pyper argues concerning the prophet Nathan, "not everything the prophet says [and does] is from God."[69] And the DH editors should not have the final say as to what should and should not be ascribed to God? Is the successful abuse of power, for example in the actualization of a curse or blessing conjured in God's name, evidence that God sanctioned the outcome and/or the abuse?[70] Can and do servants of God successfully misuse their authority and power in sacred texts? The answer is yes! Can we count on God or Goddess to always or ever intervene when an otherwise authorized person abuses or misrepresents his or her power?

Readers are not told if the boys survived the mauling or if they did what physical injuries they incurred. Elisha does not care; Yahweh does not care (as depicted), and neither are the readers expected to care. The narrator seems to think it doesn't matter, that the audience is not and would not be interested in their story since they are depicted as guilty (of a capital offense) and their guilt is inexcusable even to Yahweh. The boys are not warned or given a chance to repent, as with Jonah and Nineveh. Here, God is not characterized as long-suffering or compassionate, and neither is God's prophet. The question we as readers should ask ourselves is what acts of power and authority extend or demonstrate the love and justice of God

---

68. *Los Angeles Times*, "Hear the 911 Call about Tamir Rice."

69. Pyper, "1, 2 Samuel," 388.

70. Mercer, "Elisha's Unbearable Curse," 183. Mercer argues that a curse could only be effective if it constituted or was in line with God's will.

on the earth? Which acts manifest human abuse grounded in dominance, nationalism, conservatism (preserving one's inequitable advantage at the expense of and on the bodies of the other) and fear?

LEGITIMATE AND NORMALIZED VIOLENCE

When readers are willing to excuse violence based on the authority attributed to the perpetrator of violence and/or the subordinated status (in terms of race/ethnicity, class, gender, religious affiliation, sexuality, dis-ability, and so on) of the victim, violence can be easily normalized. Violence gets normalized when the dominant group (and/or the subordinated other) minimizes the impact of violence on the other or regards such violence as the cost of doing business. Weitzer and Tuch state that even after major scandals and independent investigations, a police department rarely undertakes significant or lasting reform.[71]

When religion or religious belief is aligned with or undergirds nationalism or nation building and preservation of dominance, power, and authority invested in peoples, places, and spaces, violence committed against the constructed other, be they women or children, is normalized. When we are repeatedly exposed to violence in our reading and re-readings of the sacred text, violence is understood as an ordinary and normal aspect of becoming the people of God. In the process of normalizing, what would otherwise be unthinkable becomes conceivable and even "de-dramatized" less dramatic, remarkable, noteworthy, or substantial.[72] Violence is normalized when it gets folded into the ordinary.[73] Violence can be normalized when we live it every day, virtually or in reality. When we ingest violence in the sacred text, in the sacred act of preaching, in classrooms and elsewhere, from week to week, with little or no disruption, protest, or critique, it gets folded into the ordinary. Normalized violence is no less painful or annihilating to its victims. Violence is normalized when we rationalize its existence, blame the victims, excuse with impunity the perpetrators, codify it and/or sacralize it, attributing some kind of sacredness to the act or to the perpetrator of the act. Or when we fail to recognize that if what is sacred can envelope and enact sinful, unjust violence. The sacralization of violence contributes to the normalization of violence. The attribution of violence

71. Weitzer and Tuch, *Race and Policing in America*, 37.

72. Baaz and Stern, "Why do Soldiers Rape?," 510.

73. Daas, "Violence, Gender and Subjectivity," 283–99.

to the divine contributes to the normalization of violence. The failure to critically read sacred texts in which violence is attributed to God or God's authorized agents, carried out with impunity, and inflicted upon persons considered more worthy of violence because of the transgression of socially constructed identities and/or perceived threats to the dominant group, contributes to the normalization of violence.

CHAPTER SEVEN

A Womanist Reading of Susanna

Patriarchal Authority, Sexual Violence, and Profiling Women of Color

In this chapter I read the apocryphal book of Susanna (a Greek addition to Daniel)[1] in dialogue with sexual harassment and violence that women of color experience from police authorities. This inter(con)textual reading places ancient (con)texts in conversation with contemporary experiences, traditions, and voices. An intersectional approach addresses the simultaneous impact of multiple social categories on Susanna and on the lives of women of color. Women of color experience the intersectional effect of oppressions based on race, gender, class, and sexuality. In conversation with the works of womanist theologian Kelly Brown Douglas, black feminist E. Francis White, comparative historian Orlando Patterson, and other pertinent voices, I discuss the commonalities, complexities, ambiguities, and dissonances in and between the story of Susanna and the experiences of African American women and other women of color. Amy-Jill Levine states that in the Hellenistic narratives, Jewish women and men, similar to men and women in the biblical canon "are rarely ideal figures: they are morally ambiguous; not always clearly motivated; torn between divine and secular interests. As individual charades, metonymies of the community, or representatives for the deity, they continue to thwart the optimistic hopes of those seeking access to the history of Jewish women and their

---

1. My translations are based on the Theodotian text dated to about the first century BCE.

communities."[2] Some readers affirm the courage Susanna displays in the narrative but consider her irredeemable as a model for empowering women to resist their own objectification and to become agents of their own liberation or to assist in transformation of gendered bias and behaviors associated with it. I argue that despite her contingent social privilege Susanna might be understood as a symbol of empowerment that resonates with some poor women of color. Some women that have been sexually violated by men that function as moral and authoritative forces in their communities resisted or exercised agency to the best of their ability. They resisted when their backs were pressed against the nearly impenetrable wall that racism, classism, heterosexism, and patriarchy built.

POLICE SEXUAL MISCONDUCT AND WOMEN OF COLOR

Policing in America is an overwhelmingly white male dominated institution, even in neighborhoods where the residents are majority people of color. Local police departments situated in majority nonwhite neighborhoods are generally not representative of the people they have been entrusted to serve and protect. Police brutality against black men and other men of color and the mentally ill has received some public attention, if very little justice, lately due to the invention of, and increased use of, cell phone cameras and social media. But comparatively little attention has been paid to police brutality and sexual misconduct against women of color and poor women. Many black women and other women of color held their breath during the trial of Oklahoma City police officer Daniel Holtzclaw, who was charged with the sexual assault and rape of poor black women. The black women Holtzclaw profiled were poor with some kind of police record and/or a history of drug abuse or of sex work. Holtzclaw's victims knew painfully well that should they tell their truth, it would be his word against theirs. After all the police (and many communities, especially majority white ones) view themselves a "moral force, protecting innocent and productive members of the public against those who would brutalize and victimize ordinary decent citizens . . . pitted against the forces of anarchy [lawlessness]."[3] The Holtzclaw trial and its outcome received little media coverage from major networks. Perhaps this silence was because of the race and class status of

2. Levine, "'Hemmed in on Every Side,'" 177.

3. Skolnick and Fyfe, *Above the Law*, 92, 93.

Holtzclaw's victims. Nevertheless, women of color followed the trial and were hoping against history for a just guilty verdict. In December 2015 we exhaled a bitter-sweet sigh of relief when a jury convicted Holtzclaw of eighteen counts of rape and sexual assaults against black women; he was sentenced to 263 years in prison.[4] It was also a bitter-sweet victory for his victims and the black community because only eight of Holtzclaw's thirty-six victims received justice.

Apparently, hundreds of police officers are terminated for sexual abuse, but only a small number face criminal charges and even less are convicted of their crimes. Some states have no policies and/or disciplinary action for officer sexual misconduct. Large states like California and New York have no system for revocation of licenses for officers engaged in sexual misconduct. In some states where officers were identified through the news media and court records as having engaged in sexual misdeeds, officers were not removed from duty.[5]

Black women and other women of color have never enjoyed the same protections as white women in America. During slavery, white enslavers enjoyed unbridled access to enslaved black women's bodies; enslavers could coerce or force black women to submit to their sexual advances or to breed with/be raped by black males to economically maintain the flow of slave labor, especially when it became illegal and more difficult to engage in the African slave trade. After slavery, black women had protection of neither police nor courts; white men could rape black women with impunity. Black women could be raped by men inside and outside of their communities with little, if any, recourse or protections. The dominant culture continued to perceive black women and other women of color as inferior and unworthy of the same respect granted to white women generally.

Poor women of color are more vulnerable to sexual violence. Women regardless of class or race are the majority victims of sexual violence. As demonstrated by an estimated 400,000 or more rape kits that go untested each year, the system seldom delivers the justice women need and deserve.[6] Women generally and poor women of color (especially African American and LGBT persons) are more vulnerable to profiling by police officers

4. Redden, "Daniel Holtzclaw."

5. Sedensky and Merchant, "AP: Hundreds of Officers Lose Licenses over Sex Misconduct."

6. Sainz, "Thousands of Rape Kits Remain Untested Across the Country."

engaged in sexual misconduct. African American women and LGBT persons are routinely profiled as sex workers, even when they are not.[7]

Daniel Holtzclaw's systematic sexual assault of poor black women began to unravel when he chose to assault a fifty-seven-year-old middle-class grandmother named Jannie Ligons. Ligons worked at a daycare center and had no criminal history. As she drove home alone from an event with friends, Holtzclaw stopped Ligons and demanded that she perform oral sex on him. The very next day Ligons reported the sexual assault. Holtzclaw had been raping black women—teenagers, mothers, and grandmothers— for about seven months before he stopped Ligons who did not fit the exact profile of his previous victims.

SUSANNA: SEXUAL PROFILING AND ATTEMPTED RAPE OF A WOMAN OF PRIVILEGE

Susanna is the story of a woman sexually profiled by two community elders that judicially governed the Jewish community in Babylon, presumably with the approval of Babylon (vv. 1, 5). Susanna is privileged in that she is married to Joakim, a very wealthy man that was also the most honored man in the community (v. 4). Joakim owns a luxurious home with an adjacent garden to which he has permitted the two elders legitimate access to perform their duties as judges (v. 6). By giving the elders access to his home, they have access to Susanna. The elders constitute a moral force within the community, presiding and arbitrating over legal and moral disputes and issues. For a specific period of time each day, Joakim's house functions as (semi-)public space for the community and elders. During the hours that the elders govern in Joakim's house, Susanna attempts to maintain some semblance privacy. She does not transgress the temporary public space over which the elders exercise moral authority, but they will gaze and slither into her private space as she walks and bathes in the garden. The garden in Joakim's house is both public and private space. From Susanna's perspective, when the elders and jurors have all gone home, the garden is her own private space.[8] When the people leave and no one is home but the slaves and Susanna, the elders secretly remain as voyeurs, peering at Susanna who is described as very beautiful (vv. 2, 7–12).

7. Antoine, "The Color of Lawlessness." See also United Nations, "In the Shadows of the War on Terror."

8. Reinhartz, "Better Homes and Gardens," 334.

Separately, the two lawless (*anomia*) elders had ample time and opportunity to sexually profile Susanna, to fix their gaze on her body, to lust after her, and to imagine and conspire how they might rape her. Rather than hold one another accountable, when the elders find out that each is planning to rape Susanna, they conspire to identify the opportune day and time (vv. 13–14). When that day and time arrives, they hide in the garden to catch Susanna bathing, naked and alone. As customary when bathing, on that day Susanna sent her slaves to retrieve items for her bath (vv. 17–18). Once the slaves close the doors, the two elders show themselves and try to coerce Susanna into submitting to rape, hoping she will agree not to resist too loudly or aggressively (vv. 19–21). Susanna chooses to yell in hopes she will be heard; she will take her chances rather than sin against the Lord (vv. 22–23). Susanna refuses to be coerced into acquiescing to rape by the pair.[9] When Susanna yells, the elders yell too, no doubt in order to confuse the people in the house (v. 24). Slinging open the doors, before anyone else opens them, the elders falsely accuse Susanna of having an affair with a young man who conveniently escapes from the house, without trace or identity (vv. 25–26). According to the elders' testimony, Susanna had dismissed her slaves so that she could be alone with her young lover (vv. 34–37). Despite the elders' false testimony, Susanna narrowly escapes capital punishment when a wise young man named Daniel intervenes, exposing the two elders a liars with a history of sexually violating the daughters of Israel (vv. 49–59).[10] Ultimately, Daniel gains a reputation as a wise elder, Joakim's honor remains intact, and Susanna is exonerated from a crime she never committed. "Ever since that day Daniel became great among the people" (v. 64).

WOMEN'S BODIES AND THE CONSTRUCTION OF COMMUNITY IDENTITY

The reputation of the community is interconnected with the reputation of the elders it chooses to represent them, and thus the community's reputation

9. I agree with Glancy ("The Accused," 104) that Susanna was not seduced as some interpreters argue but that the elders attempt to rape her. Both views are based on contemporary concerns. Glancy focuses on the construction of the elders as subject and Susanna as an object to be seen or looked at and the impact of that construction on readers.

10. Pearce ("Echoes of Eden," 19) discusses the contrast between Susanna as "daughter of Judah" and the elders as the "sons of Israel."

is dependent on Daniel as the one who exposes the community's elected elders (vv. 28, 41b, 47–50, 51, 60). Daniel's reputation is dependent on or built upon the exoneration of Susanna's reputation. Black men's reputation and manhood, as well as the dignity of the black community, historically hinged on black men's (in)ability to protect black women from sexual violence in slavery when black people had no civil rights and beyond, when black people's rights were unprotected. Black families have had to teach their daughters and sons how to survive outside and inside of their communities, as well as "how to continue the survival of the black community itself."[11] E. Frances White asserts that, "the black family has evolved into an institution that offers shelter for the black community in the face of political repression and economic depression," but on black women's backs is levied the heaviest tax for maintaining the shelter; this uneven burden will go unacknowledged as long as the imbalance of power that favors men is ignored.[12] Levine states that groups facing the challenges of diaspora living and colonialism sometimes "achieve self-identity," namely "ethnic pride, personal piety, class structure," discursively constructed or inscribed on women's bodies.[13] Three primary motifs are employed in Hellenistic texts to "represent and to counter the challenge to communal self-identity." First, women's bodies as a microcosm of the community become the contested spaces on which is imprinted "the struggles between the adorned and the stripped, the safe and the endangered, the inviolate and the penetrated."[14] Second, women's husbands portray ineptness, weaknesses, or simple stupidity. Finally, the borders of body and society are muddied "through an emphasis on boundary-transgressive events: a focus on eating, defecating, burial, and sexual intercourse as well as a confusion between public and private, privileged and marginalized."[15] Constructions of women as literary tropes allow readers to peer into social worlds that reveal more about specific historical communities than about real women's lives. "The women of the Apocrypha and Pseudepigrapha are the screen on which the fears of the (male) community—of impotence, assimilation, loss of structure—can

11. White, *Dark Continent of Our Bodies,* 70.

12. Ibid., 72.

13. Levine, "'Hemmed in on Every Side,'" 179. Reinhartz ("Better Homes and Gardens," 337) argues that the garden represents Israel and the house to which it is attached symbolizes Babylon who tries to enter the garden, but the community remains impenetrable, just as Susanna remains pure.

14. Ibid., 179.

15. Ibid.

be both displayed and, at least temporarily, allayed."[16] According to Gómez-Acebo, Susanna's context is the emergence of a new class of independent cultured elites who attempt to defend their Jewish identity.[17]

After Emancipation from American slavery, some African Americans called for a cultured or educated elite epitomized by educated, pure, and virtuous black women. For example, in 1870 Sarah Dudley, General Secretary of the Woman's Home and Foreign Missionary Society of the AME Zion Church argued that, "Womanhood and manhood begin in the cradle and around the fireside; mother's knee is truly the family altar. True patriotism, obedience and respect for law, both divine and civil, the love and yearning for the pure, the sublime and the good, all emanate from mother's personality. If mother be good, all the vices and shortcomings of the father will fail to lead the children astray; but if mother is not what she should be, all the holy influences of angels cannot save the children. I would urge then, as the first prerequisite for our work, a pure, pious and devoted motherhood."[18] Pure, educated and married women should be a community buffer for men's failings and a panacea for what ails the community. The community, Daniel, and Joakim's reputations rest on Susanna's innocence or guilt, sexual purity or promiscuity, and fidelity or infidelity to the Lord in heaven and to the Lord of her household; the community's identity is priority. "Susanna, as character and as text, carries possibilities for condemnation as well as praise, for the recognition of women's social and religious freedom as well as their confinement, for the discovery of how Judaism survived challenges to its self-definition as well as the compromise it made in this process."[19]

THE AMBIGUITY OF PRIVILEGE AND INTERSECTIONALITY

Some readers argue that Susanna's heroism or courage is mitigated by her privilege. She lives a socially and materially privileged life. Joakim, her husband, is very wealthy and the most respected in the community. Susanna's

16. Ibid., 180. Levine also argues that unlike women who assailed in Genesis and the Deuteronomistic History, women in the apocrypha and Pseudepigrapha remain physically and morally pure.

17. Gómez-Acebo, "Susanna," 277.

18. Pettey, "What Role is the Educated Negro Woman to Play," 79.

19. Levine, "'Hemmed in on Every Side,'" 178.

privilege is interconnected with the men in her life. Her life is constructed around and subsumed by the men who marry, parent, and advocate for her. The story begins: "there was a man . . . named Joakim. . . . He married [literally, he *took* a *gynaikē*) the daughter of Hilkiah. . . . Her parents were just (*dikaios*) and trained their daughter in the Torah (*nomos*) of Moses. . . . Joakim was very wealthy. . . . And the most highly esteemed of them all" (vv.1–4).[20] Susanna's subordination to the men in her life makes her vulnerable and, to a degree, the men in her life can be made vulnerable by Susanna's conduct. Susanna enjoys the lifestyle that her husband's wealth brings: a fine house with an adjacent enclosed garden (*paradeisos*), slaves (*korasioi/douloi*), good and plenty food, oils and expensive ointments, luxurious clothing, and a good reputation in the community. Three of these status markers will be used against Susanna in an attempt to rape her: fine house/garden, slaves, and her reputation. Being the wife of the wealthy and honored Joakim does not protect Susanna from patriarchal violence, sexual harassment or attempted rape. Women who do not pass the test of respectability politics may be easier prey for men of power and authority who want to sexually violate women, but any woman is vulnerable to men that rape women. Levine states that acknowledgment of "class differences provokes an entry into the critique of Susanna-as-character and thereby allows exploration of intertextually negative associations. Recognition of her marginalized position as a woman leads to the discovery of the relationship between the constructs of gender and ethnicity in Hellenistic Jewish narratives. Recognition of the value of her education, her piety, and her prayer reinstates a more positive social role for Jewish women that is often overlooked by those wedded to Christian or select rabbinic reconstructions."[21]

Susanna's fear of Yahweh is highlighted in the story. Susanna's loyalty to Yahweh is attributable to the training her parents gave her in the instruction of the Torah (cf. Deut 4:9–14). The false testimony of the two elders will carry the weight of (in)justice. Because of the education she received from her parents, Susanna is aware of the law (*nomos*). She knows that a charge can be brought and sustained against a woman or man on the testimony of two or three witnesses. If a false witness accuses someone of a crime or wrong doing, she must appear before Yahweh, and the priests and judges holding office at the time. Perjury is a capital offense (Deut 19:15–21). The

20. In the minds of early Jewish and Christian interpreters Susan's father Hilkiah was the priest of Josiah who found the book of the law (2 Kgs 22:10).

21. Levine, "'Hemmed in on Every Side,'" 190.

Deuteronomic law states that sins like adultery must be purged from the community (Deut 22:21, 22, 24).

Slut shaming or accusations of infidelity or promiscuity alone can ruin a woman's reputation and bolster a man's in many cases. But the more honored the husband, the more that is at stake for him if his wife is accused and/or convicted of sexual infidelity. When men want to protect their own reputations while sexually assaulting women, they will do so in a way that casts blame on the woman, that shows she was a willing participant; that she was not a virgin and therefore was somehow not rapeable (we will return to this idea below); or that she at least wanted *it* as badly as the men did and thus consented if only by not fighting hard enough or screaming loud enough. Susanna was also aware that the Torah states if an alleged sexual assault occurs in the city and no one hears the woman scream, it is assumed the woman did not scream loud enough and thus was a willing participant. Conversely, if the alleged sexual assault occurs in the country and nobody hears, it is assumed the woman may have indeed yelled for help but no one was in hearing distance (Deut 22:23–27). Susanna lived in the city of Babylon. Susanna did yell loudly and thereby thwarted the attempted rape. But the two elders yelled as well and quickly opening the garden doors they concocted the story that they caught Susanna in the act of adultery with a young man (vv. 24–27). If the young man whom the elders claim had sex with Susanna had been detained, both Susanna and the young man would be put to death because she is the wife of another man (Deut 22:22). Nevertheless, the Deuteronomic law is systematically biased against women conferring upon men the right to control female sexuality.[22] Susanna saw no way of escape. If she gave in, she might be subjected to a lifetime of being raped by the two and still suffer death. If she takes her chances with the community court, the assembly, it will be her word against two witnesses and she will likely be convicted, unless God intervenes. She chose the latter. Anyone and everyone who can save Susanna is depicted as male, biologically or metaphorically, even God as master (*kurios*).[23] As Nolte argues, at

22. Anderson, *Women, Ideology, and Violence*, 80.

23. Gafney ("Reading the Hebrew Bible Responsibly," 47) argues that when Moses encounter YHWH in the burning bush, Moshe, Moses translated the words spoked by the "Voice-in-the-Bush" from "I AM/WILL BE WHO I AM/WILL BE" to "lord." "The man, wrestling with the infinite mystery hidden and revealed in a name that was a statement of ontological being, and with his own cultural and social limitations, did not repeat the name given. . . . The man shifted the divine name from first to third person, introducing gender, which was not present in the original declaration. The man substituted the

stake here is the maintenance of "the internal integrity of the social structure. That was only possible through the intervention of a male God, using a male person, to protect a male-dominated society."[24] Gómez-Acebo asserts that Susanna "highlights a problematic use of the Torah, a basic pillar of Judaism, when two [male] witnesses agree to manipulate it."[25]

As in the case of Officer Daniel Holtzclaw, the elders ultimately harassed the woman through whom their crimes (*anomia*) would be unraveled. Both the two elders and Daniel Holtzclaw's systematic sexual abuse of women is disrupted by women who were considered more privileged than their previous victims. Just as Holtzclaw's victims submitted to sexual assault and rape out of fear, the daughters of Israel had submitted (v. 57). Significantly, Susanna is distinguished from the previous victims being called "a daughter of Judah" and the less privileged called "daughters of Israel." Of course, the Kingdom of Judah survived long after the Kingdom of Israel was destroyed by the Assyrians in the eighth century BCE.

Privilege shaming and flattery are not strategies for correcting society's inequalities. And privilege can be complex and ambiguous. Zack states, "To admit one has privilege . . . is to implicitly flatter oneself. . . . [The discourse of white privilege and the lack of privilege] is a distraction from effective action . . . the discourse of white privilege, alone, does not have the gravitas or urgency of either moral principle or social, institutional, and political action."[26] Further Zack argues that what nonwhites without privilege often lack is a protected right; the privilege that whites are sometimes said to have is actually a right that, "both whites and nonwhites have that is violated when nonwhites are the ones who own it."[27] White people who do not enjoy the extra perks associated with white privilege can deny that they have white privilege and thus deny the existence of profound racial inequalities in society.[28] "Privileges are usually conditional, whereas rights are unconditional."[29]

Nolte states that, "to empower Susanna into someone who could decide and speak for herself would lead to chaos in the Jewish symbolic

---

human male elite title 'lord' for 'I AM' and added hierarchy to the divine name."

24. Nolte, "A Politics of the Female Body," 155.

25. Gómez-Acebo, "Susanna," 285.

26. Zack, *White Privilege and Black Rights*, 3–4.

27. Ibid., 4.

28. Ibid., 4.

29. Ibid., 9.

world."[30] When Vashti spoke for herself and refused to allow King Aha-suerus to sexually objectify her, the chaos was temporary and controlled (Esth 1:13–22). We sometimes over and under estimate the power of voice and what voice can do. Perhaps it is the view of the privileged that sees only one way to demonstrate power and agency. Privileged women experience oppression too and the underprivileged need privileged allies willing to sacrifice privilege for justice and equity. When the oppressed resist and use their voices, the result is often a silencing; socio-historical timing and context matter. Oppressed persons need allies within their communities as well as external to them. Stacy Davis argues that, "from a womanist perspective . . . Susanna is a model for oppressed Africana women, who are often forced to be silent but who know when a timely word can lead to their redemption,"[31] as well as the redemption of others.

BEAUTY AND "(UN)RAPEABLE" WOMEN

In most ancient Hellenistic novels, the female protagonist is a beautiful, young, chaste woman who is kidnapped and in jeopardy of being raped; beautiful virginal women are depicted as the most rape-able.[32] Regardless of her elite socio-economic ties, Susanna's beauty and chastity make her an ideal female character in a tale about sexual violence and the lust of powerful men (vv. 2, 31; e.g., Tamar, 2 Sam 13; Bathsheba, 2 Sam 11:11–5). When a woman's beauty is presented as the cause of uncontrollable male lust, beautiful women, slave or free, are constructed as innately dangerous. Harriet Jacobs (aka Linda Brent), an enslaved African female in the American South, states in her slave narrative that beauty was an added curse to slave children: "If God has bestowed beauty upon her, it will prove her greatest curse. That which commands admiration in the white woman only hastens the degradation of the female slave. I know that some are too much brutalized by slavery to feel the humiliation of their position; but many slaves feel it most acutely, and shrink from the memory of it. . . . other slaves . . . knew too well the guilty practices under that roof [Mr. Flint,

30. Nolte, "A Politics of the Female Body," 156.

31. Davis, "Susanna," 312.

32. For example see *The Story of King Apollonius of Tyre* (King Antiochus of Antioch, a widower, rapes his beautiful daughter and lives with her in incestuous relationship and any suitors must solve the riddle); Xenophon's *Ephesian Tale*; Chariton's *Callirhoe and Chaereas*; and Heliodorus's *An Ethiopian Romance*.

her enslaver's plantation]; and they were aware that to speak of them was an offence that never went unpunished."[33] Upon both enslaved Africans in America, and African American women, was imposed the stereotype of the hypersexual Jezebel. Black women were a threat to white purity. Thus, "in the illogic of white cultural ideology, white men were considered the victims of black women's seductive wiles."[34] Kelly Brown Douglass writes that, "Black women were ensnared in a system that labeled them Jezebels and then compelled them into a 'promiscuous life.'"[35] In 1944 African American merchant seaman Eugene Henderson wrote a letter to Alabama Governor Sparks in which he stated, "my morale drops when I learn that a woman [Recy Taylor] of my race has been brutally raped by six-white men and nothing done about it. . . .Why isn't Negro womanhood as sacred as white womanhood?"[36] President Ronald Reagan referred to poor black women receiving public assistance as "welfare queens" (despite the fact that numerically most women on welfare were and continue to be poor white women), a sexually charged political and immoral synonym for Jezebel.

It is true that femininity is presented as "to-be-looked-at-ness" in this story,[37] but not all femininity is depicted equally so. In Susanna, the slave women are not looked at or gazed upon by the two elders (perhaps the elders had already violated them, given their predatory history). The slave girls are not depicted as beautiful, but while engaged in their duties for Susanna, they are unwittingly used by the elders. They may not be daughters of Israel or Judea, but women who have been conquered by the Babylonians. Or perhaps given Joakim's status, they were slaves that Joakim already owned when he went into exile in Babylon and was permitted to keep them. In such case, they would be doubly oppressed or marginalized. The slave girls can be sexually taken without being gazed upon; they don't have to be beautiful; they are always accessible. The dichotomies of beautiful/ugly women and good/bad women, and virtuous or chaste/promiscuous women must be challenged as a bankrupt system for classifying women.

33. Jacobs, *Incidents in the Live of a Slave Girl*, 774.

34. Douglas, *What's Faith Got to Do With It*, 170.

35. Douglas, *Sexuality and the Black Church*, 39.

36. McGuire, *At the Dark End of the Street*, 28–29. The Montgomery bus boycott often called the impetus for the modern civil rights movement was actually "the culmination of a deep history of gendered political appeals—frequently led by black veterans—for the protection of African-American women from sexual and physical assault," 51.

37. Glancy, "The Accused," 107.

The ideologies behind the dichotomies need to be exposed.[38] Women who are positioned outside of the construction of ideal womanhood and with negative labels (i.e., ugly, promiscuous, ungodly) are determined to be unrespectable.[39] White states that, "to be positioned outside the 'protection' of womanhood was to be labeled unrespectable. . . . Sexual assaults on black women perpetrated by white men continued in the postbellum period as if slavery had not ended; white men's maintenance of the right to possess black women's bodies had both immediate and far-reaching consequences. . . . White skin privilege that protected most white women from black men left black women open to attacks by these men. Virtually no protection was provided for women who were portrayed as loose and licentious."[40] Women who are characterized as Jezebels or loose, promiscuous women with hyper-libidos are always rapeable. In other words, women of color can never be considered chaste or virgins. Yet, despite the gender hierarchy and the impact of race upon gender hierarchy, membership in an elite social class or a dominant race does not make a woman immune from sexual harassment and violence. Chastity or sexual purity is always constructed in relation to men and can always be (re)defined by men or a male dominated society. Chastity and sexual purity serve the male imagination and interests.[41]

When Susanna appeared before the people gathered to hear her case, she was accompanied by her parents, children, and relatives; there was no specific mention of her husband being present until her vindication (vv. 30, 63). Perhaps, as the most honored man in the community, his show of support for Susanna would constitute a conflict of interest; his honor is at stake. In the presence of the assembly, the elders order the removal of Susanna's veil, exposing her beauty (v. 32). When she appears before the community she is described as very delicate (*tryphera sphodra*) and beautiful. Once again the elders demonstrate their obsession with Susanna's beauty. But by forcing the removal of her veil it is also possible that the elders hoped to garner the support of the community and jurors for their accusations against Susanna, since the prevailing ideology is that beautiful women are

38. White, *Dark Continent of Our Bodies*, 35.

39. Ibid., 33.

40. Ibid., 33–34.

41. For a discussion of visual art representations of Susanna in which she morphs over a long history from a model of feminine virtue and chastity to a seductress, see Bohn, "Rape and the Gendered Gaze," 259–86. See also Clanton, *The Good, the Bold, and the Beautiful*.

dangerous and seducible. Thus, it becomes plausible that a young man suc-cumbed to Susanna's beauty and she to his seduction. That Daniel never looks at Susanna may demonstrate shared acceptance of the "known dan-gers" of looking at a beautiful woman and how such a gaze ensnares men.[42]

HONOR AND SHAME

One can be humiliated or shamed by ugliness; honorable persons avoid ugliness.[43] As stated above, the first persons that hear the two elders' ac-cusations against Susanna are the other people in the house (as with Joseph and Potiphar's wife, Gen 39). The people in the house are the male and female household slaves (*douloi*), including the female slaves who helped Susanna prepare for her regular baths; they had left the room and closed the door behind them, at Susanna's command. Glancy states that slave girls, body slaves, are the only buffer, a symbolic one, between Susanna and the external world; the story depends upon their presence and absence and the shame they feel as a result of the accusations that depend on their absence. Further Glancy notes that the shame the narrator ascribes to the slave girls is ambiguous; are they ashamed of what they think of Susanna or of what other's might think? "By positing shame as the slaves' reaction to the tale the narrator assumes an identity between the interests of the mistress and the slaves."[44] The shame that the slaves feel for Susanna's predicament may signify the humanity they share in common with her and also their diverse experiences. Slaves were considered to be without honor and thus without shame; persons who claim honor and to whom honor is attributed "feel shame and dishonor."[45] Behaving honorably and "*being* honorable" are two different things; and being honored (as are cows in India) does not make a person honorable (author's italics).[46] However, slaves continue to struggle for the same dignity (honor) and freedom that slave masters enjoy. Orlando Patterson argues that, "whenever we hear the voice of the slave himself, or whenever we hear from chronicler and analysts who attempt to probe

42. Glancy, "The Accused," 110.

43. For the moralizing of honor and shame see, Lyons, "Plato's Attempt to Moralize Shame."

44. Glancy, "The Mistress—Slave Dialectic," 79–80.

45. Patterson, *Slavery and Social Death*, 79.

46. Patterson, *Slavery and Social Death*, 80. There have been instances of slaves being honored while continuing to be "despised as persons without honor."

behind planter-class ideology into the actual feelings of the slave, what invariably surfaces is the incredible dignity of the slave."[47]

Perhaps as Sarah Pearce argues, Susanna is the first Second Eve who feels no shame,[48] despite being unjustly exposed. Perhaps the slaves absorb and express all the shame; they bear it and feel it in their bodies. Perhaps in Susanna, we are afforded a glance at the humanity of the slaves. The female slave's body is constantly violated or penetrable by the slave master with impunity. From the plantations in the American South to the streets of major American cities, women of color have been sexually violated and shamed with impunity. During a 2016 visit to Texas, a friend shared with me that a young Hispanic mother confided in her that she felt ashamed because a Texas patrolman stopped her and out of fear she "compromised herself." Fearing for her life, she was coerced into having sexual relations with the policeman. The young mother carried the shame that should not be hers to bear. I shared this story with colleagues at a professional meeting, and one of them responded that he knew of a Hispanic woman who was also coerced into submitting to sexual assault by a policeman. Indeed, as Glancy states a victim of sexual assault or rape should not be considered any less a victim because she or he yields to coercion or force in order to remain alive.[49] Readers can acknowledge the courage Susanna demonstrated and "reject her moral code, which implies that the preservation of women as symbols of their father's/husband's honor is more important than the preservation of women's lives."[50] Susanna's life and well-being is tied up with her husband's honor so that protecting his honor also means safeguarding her livelihood and privilege. This is also a poor woman's predicament.

Susanna's honor is intimately linked to her husband's honor. Glancy argues that what is at stake in the story is the honor of Joakim's household and not Susanna's physical safety.[51] It is complex; if Susanna is convicted of being responsible for dishonoring her husband, and by extension his household, by sexual infidelity, she becomes physically vulnerable; she will have no protection from the penalty the law imposes. Susanna cannot claim or be honored in the same manner as her husband; but she can be dishonored (falsely accused) or honored (exonerated). The very space Susanna

47. Ibid., 100.
48. Pearce, "Echoes of Eden."
49. Glancy, "The Accused," 115.
50. Ibid., 109.
51. Ibid., 107.

seeks to save from dishonor is the same space where she is honored, not as the owner of the household but as chaste wife. To dishonor the husband who provides for her material needs would place Susanna's own livelihood in jeopardy. This is part of the problem in our contemporary society with intimate partner violence where the man is the aggressor *and* the primary provider. This is the dilemma of many women who are sexually assaulted and violated in the workplace by their male employers. Women that are sexually violated and raped by an intimate partner that is also the primary wage earner in the home are likely to remain silent about being abused, wittingly or unwittingly protecting the man's honor so that he does not lose his job. We can condemn the ideology that shames a woman if she chooses to submit to coercion instead of death. Also women should not be shamed for choosing death over rape and sexual violence.

RESISTANCE, AMBIVALENCE, AND GOD

Some enslaved women in the American South, who did not want their daughters to experience the sexual violence they endured, committed infanticide to save them from the same violence and degradation. It is not impossible for a woman herself to choose death over rape; the impact of rape could consume a rape victim's life, making it impossible for her or him to live a normal life or to engage in normal relationships. And the fear of being repeatedly raped by the same man can be unbearable, which is what Susanna might have been subjected to had she not said, "no." Clarice Martin states that the slaves' bodies bore "the visible and invisible imprints of the master's *patria potestas* [father's power]."[52] Like Susanna, enslaved African women struggled and women of color still strive to "safeguard their virtue," drawing on the "physical, intellectual, instinctual, and especially spiritual resources" at their disposal in "their attempts to escape the immoral privilege [and dominance] that white men claimed over their bodies."[53] Douglas argues we cannot underestimate the function of faith for helping black women maintain agency over their bodies. "Spirituality of resistance" is defined by a sense of connectedness to one's heritage and to the Divine; provides a defense against white ideological constructions of black men and women as "unworthy of freedom, dignity, and even life";

52. Martin, "The Eyes Have It," 222.
53. Douglas, *What's Faith Got to Do With It?*, 172.

and it provides black women with a sense of power over their own bodies as sacred.[54]

We cannot guarantee that if Susanna had told her own story the language would be any different if she did not have access to other language in resisting rape. Is the reason for resistance more important than the resistance? Should women be required to construct an ideology of liberatory resistance before engaging in resistance? In a perfect world, we might perfectly articulate the reasons for our resistance. It is easier to construct ideologies or theories about resistance than it is to resist oppression and surrender privilege with real material consequences. Resistance is not always accompanied by or based on ideological consciousness about one's oppression; a liberative ideology or conscientization may develop after the resistance or in the process, and sometimes never. Sometimes resistance is about survival. Glancy argues that Susanna "reflects and contributes to the conventional representation of gender."[55] Susanna may at times both resist and unknowingly reinscribe her gendered subordination.

Perhaps Susanna's training in the Torah, together with being the daughter of a priest, emboldened her resistance to being raped and to take her chances with Yahweh and with the patriarchal structure. Until the structure or system is changed, it is the only system to which Susanna can appeal. Sometimes education, being conscious of what the Torah teaches in Susanna's case, can embolden one to resist violence with voice and body, but not always.

WHEN GOD SEEMS COMPLICIT IN VIOLENCE

The Jewish people had appointed two elders to serve as judges over the Jewish community living in Babylon (v. 5). The omniscient narrator informs the readers that the *despotes* (master, as in slave master) had identified the two elders as wicked. Does this designation refer to Yahweh or to the colonizing/imperial masters?[56] "Concerning them the Master said to them. . . ." Who is "them"? Is it the people in general; did they know the elders were doing wicked things but kept silent? Levine asserts that the "deity is not

54. Ibid.

55. Glancy, "The Accused," 105.

56. See 1 Tim 6:1; Titus 2:9; 1 Pet 2:18 where *despotes* refers to slave masters; cf. Luke 2:29; Acts 4:24; Rev 6:10 where *despotes* refers to God or Jesus.

a voyeur," but makes an appearance only when Susanna cries out.[57] If the despotes is Yahweh, then the deity is a voyeur to some degree, it seems, since the despotes knows that the elders are lawless (*anomia*) yet does not intervene until Susanna cries out. If God is a voyeur until called upon by a "beautiful" daughter of Israel, it raises a question of theodicy about the presence of God and injustice. Does, "the Master [*despotes*] had said" mean that *God* had revealed the wickedness (*anomia*) of the elders to the people (v. 5)? From Daniel's testimony, the two elders had engaged in sexual assault and rape of the daughters of Israel/Judah for some time with impunity (v. 57). Or maybe the despotes refers to a more proximate external gaze of the colonizing masters, and ultimately Daniel through Susanna, subverts the colonial gaze by public shaming and convicting the elders.

Did the people know what the despotes knew? Were the people and their leaders complicit in the lawlessness (*anomia*)? If so, was their complicity based on a politics of disgust toward the previous victims of the elders? A politics of disgust functions to separate women (and others) of different social classes by making one class repugnant to the other by accusations and stereotypes that are accepted as plausible and believable because of a mistrust that has been encouraged and developed between persons of different socio-economic classes due to inequalities, privilege, and lack of allyship.[58] Were the other female victims considered less attractive, less reputable, regarded as promiscuous, and/or married to poor men? The impression is given that the elders were permitted to serve against the people's better judgment. Does this include Susanna and her family? Did Joakim and Susanna also know of the lawlessness behavior of the elders and still allow them to hold court in their home? Sometimes injustice committed against the other is acceptable as long as it doesn't venture into one's own yard or paradise.[59]

57. Levine, "Hemmed in on Every Side," 188.

58. See Hancock, *The Politics of Disgust.*

59. Both Levine ("Hemmed in on Every Side") and Pearce ("Echoes of Eden") acknowledge the connection between Susanna and Eve, a connection I also wish to recognize. Based on the OG or LXX version of Susanna, Pearce convincingly argues that Susanna is depicted as a first second Eve who reverses the fortunes of the first Eve. The LXX version strategically employs the language of LXX Gen 3. The Elders who are beguiled by Susanna's beauty (as serpent beguiled Eve in Paradise) are cast out of their Paradise. See also, Reinhartz, "Better Homes and Gardens."

HEAVEN, (IN)JUSTICE, AND EXONERATION

Justice as an ideal has always been partisan, favoring some groups over others and has neglected actual injustice. Naomi Zack states that, "St. Augustine and St. Aquinas represented the interests of the Catholic Church in political Christian theodicies deferring justice to heaven."[60] The narrator's explanation as to how the elders could attempt to rape Susanna is that they had silenced their consciences, averted their gaze from heaven (to Susanna's body) and did not remember their duty to administer justice (*dikaios*) (v. 9). Conversely, Susanna looked toward Heaven for justice, even as she cried, trusting the Lord (*kurios*) to intervene (v. 35). The elders repressed and ignored both the internal and external sources necessary for conscientization about injustice and for doing justice. At the intersection or nexus of love of self and love of God is love of neighbor.

Stacy Davis states that, "Susanna's words move God to act on her behalf. Susanna has a womanist's faith."[61] Faith has not always moved God, at least not in ways that stop men (and women) from molesting, raping, trafficking, and killing women and men. A downside to stories like Susanna's is that they sometimes enable readers to embrace an uncritical faith that is afraid to grapple with the hard issues of theodicy and to face the hard reality that many a woman, child, or man (womanist and feminist) has died clutching her or his faith.

When the patriarch Joseph was a slave in Pharaoh's house and Potiphar's wife tried to persuade him to submit to rape, Joseph employed the same language that Susanna used in his refusal to acquiesce (Gen 39). Joseph refuses to wrong his master for by doing so he would commit a wicked act (*rhēma ponerōn*) equivalent to sin against God (Gen 39:9).[62] Potiphar's wife lied and said that Joseph raped her, and he was sentenced to prison for an indefinite period of time. Differently, because Susanna was accountable to Jewish law, she could be stoned to death. Both Joseph and Susanna refused to dishonor their master's household and to sin against God. Both the anonymity of two elders and Potiphar's wife is protected in

60. Zack, *White Privilege and Black Rights*, 65, 66.

61. Davis, "Susanna," 313.

62. Gómez-Acebo ("Susanna") notes the similarities between Daniel and Joseph who both become important figures in the royal court of Babylon and Egypt, respectively. However, the author does not note the similarities between Potiphar's wife's attempted rape of Joseph and the elders' attempted rape of Susanna.

the narratives. In both narratives the household slaves are the first to hear the false allegations about rape (Gen 19:14–18).

In community court, the elders refer to Susanna's alleged infidelity as wickedness (*anomia*) (v. 38). After the assembly convicted Susanna on the elders' testimony, it sentenced Susanna to death (v. 41). Nolte questions why Daniel does not assist Susanna in developing her own voice.[63] This story highlights the perennial problem of the dominant powers expecting the subordinated and the vulnerable to give up their voices so that androcentric, patriarchal agendas and men's voices may prevail. Women who refuse to be silenced are accused of emasculating men—a charge with which black women are too familiar. The burden of silence is laid on the backs of women of color, by the dominant white culture and by segments of their communities, so that men of color may scale the socio-economic ladder, and hopefully bring them along.

After her sentencing, Susanna challenges God's justice. In a loud public appeal to and indictment of the omniscient, eternal, prescient God, Susanna invokes the question of theodicy: God knows the evidence is false and yet she has been sentenced to death for a crime she did not commit (vv. 42–43). This is the first time the Lord (kurios) hears and responds to her plea and emboldens Daniel to protest the injustice committed against her and to intervene in her case at the last minute (v. 44). A desperate Susanna shamed an inattentive God. Daniel craftily demonstrates that the Elders had given false testimony; they were not able to synchronize their stories in the detail of the kind of tree under which the alleged infidelity occurred (vv. 51–59). Daniel works within the current structure or system to save Susanna. Susan Sered and Samuel Cook argue that Susanna has no access to socially accepted structural power; she possesses moral strength only.[64] But until the system is changed, the oppressed need allies to negotiate and expose injustice and unjust systems. Sered and Cook argue that Daniel, as a trickster figure (a role normally reserved for females), comes to Susanna's rescue, maintaining patriarchal structures.[65] "For the people, the woman is already other, already alien, and so already guilty. Only through Daniel's

63. Nolte, "A Politics of the Female Body," 152.

64. Sered and Cooper, "Sexuality and Social Control," 44–45. Susanna's moral strength or apparent unequivocal faith in God does not move God to directly intervene to save Susanna.

65. Ibid., 46–48, 54. The authors argue that Susanna is a transitional character having similarities and differences with traditional Jewish heroines and Christian virgin martyrs.

reclamation of her does Susanna regain her righteousness and her true ethnic identity. . . . The youth becomes the wise elder; Susanna the mother becomes his dependent. And thus, the woman and the ethnos both enter safely into Daniel's charge. In turn, Daniel's case rests not on Susanna's protestation but on the elder's testimony"[66]

Daniel's win in court restores Susanna to her previous condition of vulnerability before the elders violated her by peeping at her naked body as she bathed, at the least. As Stacey Davis asserts, the depiction of a man, Daniel, as Susanna's savior, as the answer to her prayer, is expected in a context dominated by patriarchy. Further Davis argues that, "if Africana women had written the story, a woman would have been another woman's savior."[67] Perhaps Davis is right, but we must be careful to presume that all women are interested in liberation and are concerned with liberation of other women, even if they self-identify as feminists or womanists. When it comes to how much agency women should have over their bodies, women across race, class, and religion do not agree. In my online Womanist biblical hermeneutics course, a white female student asked in a discussion forum why *all* black women are pro-abortion. The student implied that all white Christian women are "pro-life" or anti-abortion and that all black women are "pro-abortion." I explained that black women are not a monolithic on this issue. On the first day of an Acts of the Apostles class that I taught one summer, a black female student entered with a petition in her hand demanding that anyone who identified as Christian should sign it! In that moment I gave a very brief lecture on the problem with essentializing Christian and black identity! All women do not think the same and all women do not desire to be free of patriarchal domination, unfortunately even when it is the "p*ssy grabbing" kind!

A victory in the courts does not translate into a triumph in the streets and in private domains we inhabit. Private and public structures founded on and maintained through patriarchalism, racism, classism, and heterosexism are not razed by a single court win. Particularly when elite males of the dominant group define and defend headship/leadership, ownership, scholarship/wisdom, and pedagogy across the private the public domains. As Martin Luther King Jr. stated, "Justice for black people will not flow into society merely from court decisions nor from fountains of political oratory. Nor will a few token decisions quell all the tempestuous yearnings

---

66. Levine, "'Hemmed in on Every Side,'" 189–90.

67. Davis, "Susanna," 313.

of millions of disadvantaged black people. White America must recognize that justice for black people [and other people of color and the poor] cannot be achieved without radical changes in the structure of our society. The comfortable, the entrenched, the privileged cannot continue to tremble at the prospect of change in the status quo."[68]

Perhaps Susanna should be remembered for exercising a woman's right to choose. At a crucible in her life, Susanna chose to exercise the limited power she had and refused to give the elders further access to her body. Even if readers don't agree with Susanna's choice, she chose. To resist or refuse in the face of unbridled power and authority is significant and empowering. While Susanna is silent, her actions speak loudly. Her refusal is sassy and it is talk-back to those men who forced her back against the wall. Sometimes it is more difficult to stand up to injustice within one's community when one's accusers or perpetrators are trusted members of the community and when to do so would be viewed as a traitorous act of airing of the community's dirty laundry. Toni Craven states that, "Susanna's story tells how a woman *within* the covenant community faced death and triumphed over adversity when threatened—not by powerful foreign officials but by supposedly trustworthy Jewish leaders."[69] Despite the author's use of Susanna to make Daniel look good, the story reminds us that people need to stand up to injustice in order for any justice to prevail.

When misogynistic men control and constitute the justice system, no women are safe; women of relative privilege are not even safe from the status quo. Susanna could cry foul; she could refuse to be violated but she cannot escape actual or virtual violence because of her subordination to all men. Sometimes the seemingly smallest act of resistance to one's own oppression can be significant. Sometimes the multiple jeopardies that a woman faces forces her to triage by responding to the most imminent threat that from her perspective carries the grimmest consequences for her quality of life. Persons who do not know the trauma imposed by the daily onslaught of interlocking forms of oppression might underestimate the significance of any resistance from the most vulnerable. Sometimes resistance is choosing to believe that God will make a way somehow, that God will make a way out of no way. We cannot confuse resistance with the work of transformation. The actual dismantling of oppressive structures cannot be accomplished on the back of a single woman; it will take communities banning together

68. King, *A Testament of Hope,* 314.
69. Craven, "Daniel and Its Additions," 194.

to eradicate injustice and unjust structures. As Monica Coleman argues, it is not the Savior's job or duty to make a way out of no way.[70] Change requires a communal effort. "Although saviors are the individuals who lead our communities of creative transformation, a way out of no way is too much for any one woman."[71]

70. Coleman, *Making a Way Out of No Way*, 167.
71. Ibid., 167–68.

Bibliography

Alexander, Michelle. *The New Jim Crow: Incarceration in an Age of Color Blindness*. New York: New, 2012.

Alter, Robert. *The Art of Biblical Narrative*. New York: Basic, 1981.

———. "Biblical Type Scenes and the Uses of Convention." *Critical Inquiry* 5 2 (1978) 355–68.

Anderson, Cheryl B. *Women, Ideology, and Violence. Critical Theory and the Construction of Gender in the Book of the Covenant and the Deuteronomic Law*. New York: T&T Clark, 2004.

Anderson, Robert T. "Mount Gerizim: Navel of the World." *The Biblical Archaeologist* 43 4 (1980) 217–21.

Andrade, Nathanael. "Ambiguity, Violence, and Community in the Cities of Judea and Syria." *Historia: Zeitschrift für Alte Geschichte* 59 (2010) 343–70.

Angelou, Maya. "Still I Rise." *Phenomenal Woman: Four Poems Celebrating Women*. New York: Random House, 1995.

Antoine, Chagmion. "The Color of Lawlessness: Sexual Abuse by Police, Nationwide." May 4, 2016. *Women's Media Center*, www.womenundersiegeproject.org/blog/entry/the-color-of-lawlessness-sexual-abuse-by-police-nationwide.

Baaz, Maria Eriksson, and Maria Stern. "Why do Soldiers Rape? Masculinity, Violence, and Sexuality in the Armed Forces in the Congo (DRC)." *International Studies Quarterly* 53 2 (2009) 495–518.

Bailey, Sarah Pulliam. "White Evangelicals Voted Overwhelmingly for Donald Trump, Exit Polls Show." *Washington Post*. November 9, 2016. https://www.washingtonpost.com/news/acts-of-faith/wp/2016/11/09/exit-polls-show-white-evangelicals-voted-overwhelmingly-for-donald-trump/?utm_term=.8213e70a7afc.

Bakhtin, Mikhail M. "Discourse in the Novel." *The Dialogic Imagination*. Austin: The University of Texas Press, 1981.

Barlow, Maude, and Tony Clarke. "Water Privatization." *Global Policy Forum*. Polaris Institute. January 2004. https://www.globalpolicy.org/component/content/article/209/43398.html.

Beasley-Murray, George R. *John*. Edited by Ralph Martin. Vol. 36: WBC: Waco, TX: Word, 1987.

Bhabha, Homi K. *The Location of Culture*. London and New York: Routledge, 1994.

———. "The Other Question. Stereotype, Discrimination and the Discourse of Colonialism." In *The Location of Culture*, edited by Homi K. Bhabha, 94–120. New York: Routledge, 1994.

Black, Max. *Metaphors: Studies in Language and Philosophy*. Ithaca: Cornell University Press, 1962.

Bohn, Babette. "Rape and the Gendered Gaze: *Susanna and the Elders* in Early Modern Bologna." *Biblical Interpretation* 9 (2001) 259–86.

Boring, Eugene. *Gospel of Matthew*. In *NIB*, edited by Leander Keck. Nashville: Abingdon, 1995.

Boyd, Gregory A. *Repenting of Religion: Turning from Judgment to the Love of God*. Grand Rapids: Baker, 2004.

Burnett, Joel S. "'Going Down' to Bethel: Elijah and Elisha in the Theological Geography of the Deuteronomistic History." *Journal of Biblical Literature* 129 2 (2010) 281–97.

Burrus, Virginia. "The Gospel of Luke and the Acts of the Apostles." *A Postcolonial Commentary on the New Testament Writings*, edited by F. F. Segovia and R.S. Sugirtharajah, 133–55. London: T&T Clark, 2007.

Byron, Gay L. *Symbolic Blackness and Ethnic Difference in Early Christian Literature*. New York/London: Routledge, 2002.

Byron, Tammy K. "'A Catechism for Their Special Use': Slave Catechisms in the Antebellum South." PhD Diss. University of Arkansas, 2008.

Cannon, Katie Geneva. *Katie's Canon: Womanism and the Soul of the Black Community*. New York: Continuum, 1995.

Carter, Warren. "The Gospel of Matthew." *A Postcolonial Commentary of the New Testament Writings*, edited by Fernando F. Segovia and R.S. Sugirtharajah, 69–103. New York: T&T Clark, 2009.

———. *Matthew and the Margins: A Socio-Political and Religious Reading*. Sheffield: Sheffield, 2000.

Chapman, Mary M. "Detroit Shuts Off Water to Residents But Not to Businesses Who Owe Millions." *The Daily Beast*. July 26, 2014. http://www.thedailybeast.com/articles/2014/07/26/detroit-shuts-off-water-to-residents-but-not-to-businesses-who-owe-millions.html.

Chesnutt, Charles. "Lynching Statistics." *Charles Chesnutt Digital Archives*. (1999) http://www.chesnuttarchive.org/classroom/lynchingstat.html.

Chiappetta, Michael. "Historiography and Roman Education." *History of Education Journal* 4 4 (1953) 149–56.

Choi, Jin Young. *Postcolonial Discipleship of Embodiment: An Asian and Asian American Feminist Reading of the Gospel of Mark*. New York: Palgrave Macmillan, 2015.

Coates, Ta-Nehisi. *Between the World and Me*. New York: Spiegel & Grau, 2015.

Coleman, Monica A. *Making a Way Out of No Way: A Womanist Theology*. Minneapolis: Fortress, 2008.

Collins, Patricia Hill. *Fighting Words: Black Women and the Search for Justice*. Minneapolis: University of Minnesota Press, 1998.

Craven, Toni. "Daniel and Its Additions." *The Women's Bible Commentary*, edited by Carol A. Newsom and Sharon H. Ringe, 191–94. Louisville: Westminster John Knox, 1992.

Dahl, N. A. "Nations in the New Testament." *New Testament Christianity for Africa and the World: Essays in Honor of Harry Sawyerr*, edited by M. E. Glasswell and E. W. Fasholé-Luke. London: SPCK, 1974.

Das, Veena. "Violence, Gender, and Subjectivity." *Annual Review of Anthropology* 37 (2008) 283–99.

Daube, David. "Jesus and the Samaritan Woman: The Meaning of συγχραομαι." *Journal of Biblical Literature* 69 2 (1950) 137–47.

Davey, Monica. "Bankruptcy Lawyer is Name to Manage an Ailing Detroit." *The New York Times*. March 14, 2013. http://www.nytimes.com/2013/03/15/us/gov-rick-snyder-kevyn-orr-emergency-manager-detroit.html.

Davis, Stacy. "Susanna." *The Africana Bible.*, edited by Hugh R. Page Jr., 312–13. Minneapolis: Fortress, 2010.

Deutsch, Celia. "Wisdom in Matthew: Transformation of a Symbol." *Novum Testamentum* 32 (1990) 13–47.

DeVries, Simon J. *1 Kings. Second Edition. WBC.* Vol 12. Nashville: Thomas Nelson, 2003.

Dewey, Joanna. "The Gospel of Mark." In *Searching the Scriptures. Volume Two: A Feminist Commentary*, edited by Elisabeth Schüssler Fiorenza, 470–509. New York: Crossroad, 1998.

Dibelius, Martin. *Studies in the Acts of the* Apostles. Translated by M. Ling and Paul Schubert, edited by Heinrich Greeven. New York: Charles Scribner's Sons, 1956.

Dickey, Ariana. "Obama 'Between Two Ferns,' Kevin Bacon, Baby Tigers and More Viral Videos." *The Daily Beast.* (March 15, 2014) http://www.thedailybeast.com/articles/2014/03/15/obama-between-two-ferns-kevin-bacon-baby-tigers-and-more-viral-videos.html?source=dictionary.

Douglas, Kelly Brown. *Sexuality and the Black Church: A Womanist Perspective.* Maryknoll, NY: Orbis, 1999.

———. *Stand Your Ground. Black Bodies and the Justice of God.* Maryknoll, NY: Orbis, 2015.

———. *What's Faith Got to do With It? Black Bodies/Christian Souls.* Maryknoll, NY; Orbis, 2005.

Douglas, Mary. *Purity and Danger: An Analysis of the Concepts of Pollution and Taboo.* London and New York: Routledge, 1984.

Douglass, Frederick. *My Bondage, My Freedom.* 1855 Edition. New York: Dover, 1969.

———. *Narrative of the Life of Frederick Douglass, an American Slave, Written by Himself.* In *Slave Narratives*, edited by William L. Andrews and Henry Louis Gates Jr., 267–38. New York: Library of America, 2000.

Dube, Musa. *Postcolonial Feminist Interpretation of the Bible.* St. Louis: Chalice, 2000.

DuBois, Page. *Torture and Truth. The New Ancient World.* New York: Routledge, 1991.

Dunn, James G. *Acts of the Apostles.* Valley Forge, PA: Trinity, 1996.

Durkee, Alison. "Here's the Breakdown of How African-Americans Voted in the 2016 Election." *Mic.* November 14, 2016. https://mic.com/articles/159402/here-s-a-break-down-of-how-african-americans-voted-in-the-2016-election#.7wtw9uBcp.

Edwards, Breanna. "Woman Who Caused Emmitt Till's Death Admits to Lying." January 27, 2017. http://www.theroot.com/woman-who-caused-emmett-tills-death-admits-to-lying-1791698393.

Ellis, Ralph, and Bill Kirkos. "Officer who Shot Philando Castile Found Guilty on All Counts." *CNN.* June 16, 2017. http://www.cnn.com/2017/06/16/us/philando-castile-trial-verdict/index.html.

Everitt, Anthony. *Cicero: The Life and Times of Rome's Greatest Politician.* New York: Random House, 2003.

Eyre, J. J. "Roman Education in the Late Republic and Early Empire." *Greece & Rome* 10 1 (1963) 47–59.

Fagan, Brian. *Elixir: A History of Water and Humankind.* New York: Bloomsbury, 2011.

Fanon, Frantz. *Black Skins, White Masks*: New York: Grove, 1967.

Bibliography

Fausset, Richard, and Ashley Southall. "Video Shows Officer Flipping Student in South Carolina, Prompting Inquiry." *New York Times*. October 26, 2015. https://www.nytimes.com/2015/10/27/us/officers-classroom-fight-with-student-is-caught-on-video.html?_r=0.

Filson, Jackie. "After Years of Crisis Detroit Residents are Demanding Affordable Water Legislation." *Food and Water Watch*. June 20, 2017. https://www.foodandwaterwatch.org/news/after-years-crisis-detroit-residents-are-demanding-affordable-water-legislation-now.

Fiorenza, Elisabeth Schüssler. *In Memory of Her: A Feminist Theological Reconstruction of Christian Origins*. New York: Crossroad, 1994.

———. *Jesus Miriam's Child, Sophia's Prophet: Critical Issues in Feminist Christology*. New York: Continuum, 1995.

Fitzmyer, Joseph A. *The Acts of the Apostles*. Anchor Bible. Vol. 31. New York: Doubleday, 1998.

Foskett, Mary F. *A Virgin Conceived: Mary and Classical Representations of Virginity*. Bloomington: Indiana University Press, 2002.

Freire, Paulo. *The Pedagogy of the Oppressed*. New York: Continuum, 1997.

Gafney, Wil. "Reading the Hebrew Bible Responsibly." In *The Africana Bible*, edited by Hugh Page, 45–51. Minneapolis: Fortress, 2010.

Garnsey, Peter. *Ideas of Slavery from Aristotle to Augustine*: Cambridge: Cambridge University Press, 1996.

Gaventa, Beverly Roberts. *From Darkness to Light: Aspects of Conversion in the New Testament*. Philadelphia: Fortress, 1986.

Glancy, Jennifer A. "The Accused. Susanna and Her Readers." *JSOT* 18 58 (1993) 103–16.

———. "The Mistress—Slave Dialectic: Paradoxes of Slavery in Three LXX Narratives." *Journal for the Study of the Old Testament* 72 (1996) 71–87

———. *Slavery in the Early Church*. Minneapolis: Fortress, 2006.

Glenn, Paul F. "The Politics of Truth: Power in Nietzsche's Epistemology." *Political Research Quarterly* 57 4 (2004) 575–83.

Gomes, Jules. "Nation and Temple: Israelite nationalism and the Sanctuary of Bethel." *Nationalism and Hindutva: A Christian Response*, edited by Mark T.B. Laing, 215–29. CMS/UBS/ISPCK, 2005.

———. *The Sanctuary of Bethel and the Configuration of Israel Identity*. Berlin/New York York: Walter de Gruyter, 2006.

Gómez-Acebo, Isabel. "Susanna, Example of Virtue and Daniel's Female Counterpart." *Escrito y otros libros sapienciales (The Writings and Later Wisdom Books)*, edited by Christ M. Maier, 275–87. Atlanta: Society of Biblical Literature Press, 2014.

Gosling, W. F. "Pets in Classical Times." *Greece & Rome* 4 (1935) 109–13.

Gosse, Dave. "Examining the Promulgation and Impact of the Great Commission in the Caribbean, 1942–1970: A Historical Analysis." *Teaching All Nations*, 33–56.

Griffin, Kimberly A., *et al.* "Digging Deeper: Exploring the Relationship between Mentoring, Developmental Interactions, and Student Agency." *Mentoring as Transformative Practice: Supporting Student and Faculty Diversity*, edited by Caroline S. Turner, 13–22. San Francisco: Jossey-Bass, 2015.

Guillen, Joe. "Detroit City Council Approves 8.7% Water Rate Increase." *Detroit Free Press*. June 17, 2014. http://archive.freep.com/article/20140617/NEWS01/306170107/City-Council-water-rate-hike.

Haenchen, Ernst. *The Acts of the Apostles*. Philadelphia: Westminster, 1971.

Hancock, Ange-Marie. *The Politics of Disgust. The Public Identity of the Welfare Queen.* New York/ London: New York University, 2004.

Hanson, Paul D. *A Political History of the Bible in America.* Louisville: Westminster John Knox, 2015.

Harrill, J. Albert. "The Psychology of Slaves in the Gospel Parables: A Case Study in Social History." *Biblische Zeitschrift* 55 (2011) 63–74.

Harris, Fredrick, and Robert Lieberman. *Beyond Discrimination, Racial Inequality in a Postracist Era.* New York: Russell Sage, 2013.

Helms, Matt. *Detroit Free Press.* "Canadians Deliver Water to Protest Detroit Shutoffs." *USA Today News* (July 26, 2014). http://www.usatoday.com/story/news/nation/2014/07/24/canadians-deliver-water-to-protest-detroit-shutoffs/13130625/.

Heschel, Abraham. *The Prophets.* New York: Harper, 2001.

Higgs, Liz Curtis. "The Woman at the Well: Thirsty for Truth, John 4:5–42." *Today's Christian Woman,* July 2008. http://www.todayschristianwoman.com/site/utilities/print.html?type=article&id=58144.

Hippolytus of Rome. "Appendix to His Works: Containing Dubious and Spurious Pieces." XLII, 53 *Ante-Nicene Fathers, Appendix* Vol. 5, edited by Alexander Roberts and James Donaldson, 252–53. Peabody, MA: Hendrickson, 1995.

Hobbs, T. R. "2 Kings." *Word Biblical Commentary. Vol 13:* Taco, TX: Word Books, 1985.

Homer. *The Iliad.* Translated by Richmond Lattimore. Chicago: University of Chicago Press, 1951.

hooks, bell. *Sisters of the Yam: Black Women and Self-Recovery.* Cambridge, MA: South End, 2005.

———. *Talking Back.* Boston: South End, 1989.

Irwin, Brian P. "The Curious Incident of the Boys and the Bears: 2 Kings 2 and the Prophetic Authority of Elisha." *Tyndale Bulletin* 67 1 (2016) 23–35.

Jacobs, Harriet. *Incidents in the Live of a slave Girl: Written by Herself.* In *Slaves Narratives,* edited by William L. Andrews and Henry Louis Gates Jr., 743–948. New York: Library of America, 2000.

Jervell, Jacob. *Die Apostelgeschichte.* Göttingen: Vendenhoeck & Ruprecht, 1998.

Jones, Rick, and Damian Robinson. "Water, Wealth, and Social Status at Pompeii: The House of the Vestals in the First Century." *American Journal of Archaeology* 109 4 (2005) 695–710.

Joseph, Gloria. "Black Feminist Pedagogy and Schooling in Capitalist White America." *Words of Fire: An Anthology of African-American Feminist Thought,* edited by Beverly Guy-Sheftall, 463–71. New York: The New Press, 1995.

Josephus. *Jewish Antiquities.* 20.44–46.

Kállay, Géza. "Some Philosophical Problems about Metaphor." *Argumentum* 10 (2014) 339–45.

Kaur, Rupi. *Milk and Honey.* Kansas City, MO: Andrews McMeel, 2015.

Khadaroo, Stacy Teicher. "Racial Gap in Discipline Found in Preschool, US Data Show." *Christian Science Monitor* (March 21, 2014). http://www.csmonitor.com/USA/Education/2014/0321/Racial-gap-in-discipline-found-in-preschool-US-data-show.

Kim, Yung Suk. *Truth, Testimony, and Transformation: A Reading of the "I Am" Sayings of Jesus in the Fourth Gospel.* Eugene, OR: Cascade, 2014.

King, Martin Luther Jr. *A Testament of Hope: The Essential Writings and Speeches of Martin Luther King, Jr.* Edited by James M. Washington. New York: HarperSanFrancisco, 1986.

———. *Stride Toward Freedom*. New York: HarperSanFrancisco, 1986.

Koester, Craig R. "'The Savior of the World' (John 4:42)." *Journal of Biblical Literature* 109 4 (1990) 665–80.

Koester, Helmut. *Introduction to the New Testament, Volume 1. History, Culture and Religion of the Hellenistic Age*. Second Edition. Berlin: Walter de Gruyter, 1995.

Lazenby, Francis D. "Greek and Roman Household Pets." *The Classical Journal* 44 (1949) 245–52.

Levine, Amy-Jill. "Gospel of Matthew." *Women's Bible Commentary: Twentieth-Anniversary Edition. Revised and Updated*. Edited by Carol A. Newsom, et al., 465–77. Louisville: Westminster John Knox, 2012.

———. "'Hemmed in on Every Side': Jews and Women in the Book of Susanna." In *Reading from this Place: Social Location and Biblical Interpretation in the United States*, edited by Fernando F. Segovia and Mary Ann Tolbert, 175–98. Minneapolis: Fortress, 1995.

Lewis, Tamar. "Black Students Face More Discipline, Data Suggests." *New York Times* (March 6, 2012). http://www.nytimes.com/2012/03/06/education/black-students-face-more-harsh-discipline-data-shows.html.

Los Angeles Times Staff. "Hear the 911 Call about Tamir Rice." *Los Angeles Times* (November 26, 2014). http://www.latimes.com/nation/nationnow/la-na-nn-tamir-rice-911-call-20141126-htmlstory.html.

Lorde, Audre. "A Litany for Survival." *The Black Unicorn: Poems*. New York: W. W. Norton, 1995.

Luger, Dawn. "New Jersey Passes Bill Requiring Schools to Teach Kids How to Interact with Police." *Activist Post* (June 26, 2017). http://www.activistpost.com/2017/06/new-jersey-passes-bill-requiring-schools-teach-kids-interact-police.html.

Lyons, Dan. "Plato's Attempt to Moralize Shame." *Philosophy* 86:337 (2011) 353–74.

Macias, Kelly. "15-Year-Old Unarmed Honor Study Shot and Killed Leaving House Party By Rifle-Wielding Cop." *The Daily Kos* (May 1, 2017). http://www.dailykos.com/story/2017/5/1/1657907/-15-year-old-unarmed-high-school-student-shot-by-rifle-wielding-cop-as-he-leaves-house-party.

Marcus, David. *From Balaam to Jonah: Anti-Prophetic Satire in the Hebrew Bible*. Brown Judaic Studies 301. Atlanta: Scholars, 1995.

Marianne, Kartzow B., and Halvor Moxnes. "Complex Identities: Ethnicity, Gender and Religion, in the Story of the Ethiopian Eunuch (Acts 8:26–40)." *Religion & Theology* 17 (2010) 184–204.

Marshall, I. Howard. *Acts of the Apostles*. Grand Rapids: William B. Eerdmans, 1980.

Martin, Clarice J. "A Chamberlain's Journey and the Challenge of Interpretation for Liberation." *Semeia* 47 (1989).

———. "The Eyes Have It. Slaves in the Communities of Christ-believers." *People's History of Christianity: Christian Origins*, edited by Richard A. Horsley, 221–39. Minneapolis: Fortress, 2005.

Matthews, Shelley. *First Converts: Rich Pagan Women and the Rhetoric of Mission in Early Judaism and Christianity*. Stanford: Stanford University Press, 2001.

Mazza, Ed. "Jerry Falwell, Jr. Calls Donald Trump' the Dream President' for Evangelicals." *The Huffington Post* (April 30, 2017). http://www.huffingtonpost.com/entry/jerry-falwell-jr-dream-president-trump_us_5906950fe4b05c3976807a08.

McCall, Emmanuel. "Neither Gerizim nor Zion: Worship Beyond Race (John 4:1–42)." *Review & Expositor* 108 (2011) 585–91.

Bibliography

McGuire, Danielle L. *At the Dark End of the Street*. New York: Vintage, 2010.

Mcleod, Jonathan. "Life-Changing Encounters with Jesus: The Woman at the Well." *SermonCentral*, March 2008. http://www.sermoncentral.com/sermons.life-changing-encounters-with-jesus-the-woman-at-the-well-jonathan-mcleod-sermon-on-lordship-of-christ-119403.asp.

Mercer, Mark. "Elisha's Unbearable Curse: A Study of 2 Kings 2:23–25." *African Journal of Evangelical Theology* 21:2 (2002) 165–98.

Methodius. *Banquet of the Ten Virgins*. "The Parable of the Virgins." Discourse VI, Chapter III, 330; Discourse VII, Chapter I, 331.

Moloney, Francis J. *John*. Edited by Daniel J. Harrington. Vol. 4. Collegeville, MN: Liturgical, 1998.

Nash, R. J. *Liberating Scholarly Writing: The Power of Personal Narrative*. New York: Teachers College, 2004.

Neely, Cheryl L. *You're Dead So What? Media, Policy, and the Invisibility of Black Women as Victims of Homicide*. East Lansing, MI: Michigan State University Press, 2015.

Nelavala, Surekha. "Smart Syrophoenician Woman: A Dalit Feminist Reading of Mark 7:24–31." *Expository Times* 118 (2006) 64–69.

Nolan, Dan, and Chris Amico. "How Bad is the Opioid Epidemic." *Frontline* (February 23, 2016) http://www.pbs.org/wgbh/frontline/article/how-bad-is-the-opioid-epidemic/.

Nolte, S. Philip. "A Politics of the Female Body. Reading Susanna (LXX Additions to Daniel) in a Brutalized South African Society." *Biblische Notizen* 168 (2016) 147–61.

Norton, Yolanda. "Silenced Struggles for Survival: Finding Life in Death in the Book of Ruth." *I Found God in Me: A Womanist Biblical Hermeneutics Reader*, edited by Mitzi J. Smith, 266–80. Eugene, OR: Cascade, 2015.

O'Day, Gail R. *Gospel of John*. Edited by Leander E. Keck. Vol. IX. NIB: Nashville: Abingdon, 1995.

Okure, Teresa. "Jesus and the Samaritan Woman (JN 4:1–42) in Africa." *Theological Studies* 70 (2009) 401–18.

Okyere-Manu, Beatrice. "Colonial Mission and the Great Commission in Africa." *Teaching All Nations*, edited by Mitzi Smith, 15–32.

Omolade, Barbara. *The Rising Song of Africa American Women*. New York: Routledge, 1994.

Opie and Andy. "Sassy Fat Black Girl Witness @ Trayvon Martin Trial." June 27, 2013. https://www.youtube.com/watch?v=r5a5yaTxNpA.

Patterson, Orlando. *Slavery and Social Death: A Comparative Study*. London: Harvard University Press, 1982.

Pearce, Sarah. "Echoes of Eden in the Old Greek of Susanna." *Feminist Theology* 11 (1996) 10–31.

Perry, Aaron. "Lift up the Lowly and Bring Down the Exalted: Gender Studies, Organizations, and the Ethiopian Eunuch." *Journal of Religious Leadership* 14 1 (2015) 45–66.

Pervo, Richard I. *The Acts of the Apostles*. Hermeneia: Minneapolis: Fortress, 2009.

Pettey, Sarah Dudley. "What Role is the Educated Negro Woman to Play in the Uplifting of Her Race?" *Can I Get a Witness? Prophetic Religious Voices of African American Women: An Anthology*, edited by Marcia Y. Riggs. Maryknoll, NY: Orbis, 1997.

Plutarch. "Life of Caesar." *Parallel Lives*.

———. "Life of Cicero." *Parallel Lives*.

———. "Life of Romulus." *Parallel Lives*. Translated by Bernadotte Perrin. Loeb Classical Library 1. Cambridge: Harvard University Press, 1914.

Powery, Emerson B. "The Gospel of Mark." *True to Our Native Land,* edited by Brian Blount, 121–57. Minneapolis: Fortress, 2007.

Pyke, Alan. "Detroit Shuts off Water to Thousands of Broke Residents." *ThinkProgress. org.* June 23, 2014. http://thinkprogress.org/economy/2014/06/20/3451488/detroit-water-shutoffs-complaint/.

Pyper, Hugh S. "1, 2 Samuel." *Fortress Commentary on the Bible,* edited by Gale A. Yee, et al., 361–99. Minneapolis: Fortress, 2014.

Redden, Molly. "Daniel Holtzclaw: Former Oklahoma City Police Officer Guilty of Rape." December 10, 2015." The Guardian. https://www.theguardian.com/us-news/2015/ dec/11/daniel-holtzclaw-former-oklahoma-city-police-officer-guilty-rape. Accessed May 22, 2017.

Reimer, Ivoni Richter. *Women in the Acts of the Apostles: A Feminist Liberation Perspective.* Minneapolis: Fortress, 1995.

Reinhartz, Adele. "Better Homes and Gardens: Women and Domestic Space in the Books of Judith and Susanna." *Text and Artifact in the Religions of Mediterranean Antiquity: Essays in Honour of Peter Richardson,* edited by Stephen G. Wilson and Michel Desjardins, 325–39. Waterloo, ON: Wilfred Laurier University Press, 2000.

———. "The Gospel of John." *Searching the Scriptures,* edited by Elisabeth Schüssler. New York: Crossroad, 1998.

———. "John 4:7–42 Samaritan Woman." In *Women in Scripture,* edited by Carol Meyers. Grand Rapids, MI: Wm. B. Eerdmans, 2001.

Rice, A. J. "The Neocolonial City: Detroit and Black Political Power." Paper presented at the Annual Meeting of the 37th Annual National Council for Black Studies, The Westin Hotel—Downtown, Indianapolis, IN. March 13, 2013. http://citation. allacademic.com/meta/p_mla_apa_research_citation/6/4/8/4/1/p648413_index. html#get_document.

Rodger, A. F. "Peculium." *The Oxford Classical Dictionary, Third Edition,* edited by S. Hornblower and A. Spawforth. New York: Oxford University Press, 1996.

Russaw, Kimberly D. "Wisdom in the Garden: The Woman of Genesis 3 and Alice Walker's *Sophia*." *I Found God in Me: A Womanist Biblical Hermeneutics Reader,* edited by Mitzi J. Smith, 222–34. Eugene, OR: Cascade, 2015.

Saint Augustine of Hippo. "The Works of St. Augustin. Sermon XLIII: 1–3, 15." *Nicene and Post-Nicene Fathers: Vol. 6: Augustin: Sermon on the Mount, Harmony of the Gospels, Homilies on the Gospels,* edited by Philip Schaff, 402. Peabody, MA: Hendrickson, 2004.

Saint Clair, Raquel. "Womanist Biblical Interpretation." *True to Our Native Land, edited* by Brian Blount, 54–62. Minneapolis: Fortress, 2007.

Sainz, Adrian. *Associated Press.* "Thousands of Rape Kits Remain Untested Across the Country," CBS News, February 23, 2014. www.cbsnews.com/news/thousands-of-rape-kits-remain-untested-across-the-country/.

Salazar, María del Carmen. "A Humanizing Pedagogy: Reinventing the Principles and Practice of Education as a Journey Toward Liberation." *Review of Research in Education* 37 (2013) 121–48.

Salzman, James. *Drinking Water: A History.* London: Overlook Duckworth, 2012.

Sanchez, Ray. *CNN.* "What We Know About the Controversy in Sandra Bland's Death." http://www.cnn.com/2015/07/21/us/texas-sandra-bland-jail-death-explain/.

Sedensky, Matt, and Nomaan Merchant. "AP: Hundreds of Officers Lose Licenses Over Sex Misconduct." *Associated Press* (November 1, 2015). https://apnews.com/fd1d4d05e561462a85abe50e7eaed4ec/ap-hundreds-officers-lose-licenses-over-sex-misconduct.

Segovia, Fernando F. "Introduction: Configurations, Approaches, Findings, Stances." *A Postcolonial Commentary of the New Testament Writings*, 1–68.

———. "Postcolonial Criticism and the Gospel of Matthew." *Methods for Matthew*, edited by Mark Allan Powell, 194–238. Cambridge, UK: Cambridge University Press, 2009.

Seneca. *Ad Lucilum Epistulae Morales*. Translated by J.W. Basore. Loeb Classical Library 47. Cambridge: Harvard University Press, 1979.

Seow, Choon-Leong. "2 Kings." *New International Bible Commentary*. Vol 3. Nashville: Abingdon, 1994.

Sered, Susan, and Samuel Cooper. "Sexuality and Social Control: Anthropological Reflection on the Book of Susanna." *The Judgment of Susanna: Authority and Witness*, edited by Ellen Spolsky, 43–55. Atlanta: Society of Biblical Literature, 1996.

Sheriff, Natasja. "US Cited for Police Violence, Racism in Scathing UN Review on Human Rights." *Aljazeera America* (May 11, 2015). http://america.aljazeera.com/articles/2015/5/11/us-faces-scathing-un-review-on-human-rights-record.html.

Silva, Daniella. "Sandra Bland's Mother Speaks Out on Sandra Bland's Life, Investigation." July 23, 2015. http://www.nbcnews.com/news/us-news/sandra-blands-mother-speaks-out-daughters-life-investigation-n397576.

Sirvent, Roberto. *Embracing Vulnerability: Human and Divine*. Eugene, OR: Pickwick, 2014.

Skinner, Matthew L. *Intrusive God, Disruptive Gospel: Encountering the Divine in the Book of Acts*. Grand Rapids, MI: Brazos, 2015.

Skolnick, Jerome, and James Fyfe. *Above the Law: Police and the Excessive Use of Force*. New York: Free, 1993.

Smith, Abraham. "A Second Step in African Biblical Interpretation: A Generic Reading Analysis of Acts 8:26–40." *Reading from this Place, Vol. 1, Social Location and Biblical Interpretation in the United States*, edited by Fernando F. Segovia and Mary Ann Tolbert, 213–28. Minneapolis: Fortress, 1995.

Smith, Mitzi J. *The Literary Construction of the Other in the Acts of the Apostles: Charismatics, the Jews and Women*. Princeton Theological Monograph Series 154. Eugene, OR: Pickwick, 2011.

———. "Race, Gender, and the Politics of 'Sass': Reading Mark 7:24–30 Through a Womanist Lens of Intersectionality and Inter(con)textuality." *Womanist Interpretations of the Bible: Expanding the Discourse*, edited by Gay L. Byron and Vanessa Lovelace, 95–112. Atlanta: Society of Biblical Literature, 2016.

———. "Slavery, Torture, Systemic Oppression, and Kingdom Rhetoric: An African American Reading of Matthew 25:1–13." *Insights from African American Interpretation*. Minneapolis: Fortress, 2017.

———. "US colonial Missions to African Slaves: Catechizing black Souls, Traumatizing the Black Psychē." *Teaching All Nations. Interrogating the Matthean Great Commission*, edited by Mitzi J. Smith and Lalitha Jayachitra, 57–85. Minneapolis: Fortress, 2014.

———, ed. *I Found God in Me: A Womanist Biblical Hermeneutics Reader*. Eugene, OR: Cascade, 2015.

Solon, Pablo. "UN Declares Water as Human Right." *ClimateandCapitalism.com.* July 28, 2010. http://climateandcapitalism.com/2010/07/28/un-declares-water-a-human-right/.

Spencer, Scott F. *The Portrait of Philip in Acts.* Sheffield: JSOT, 1992.

Stade, Bernhard. *The Book of Kings: Critical Edition of the Hebrew Text, The Sacred Books of the OT.* Leipzig: J C. Hinrich, 1904.

State and County QuickFacts. Detroit (city of), Michigan. US Census Bureau. http://quickfacts.census.gov/qfd/states/26/2622000.html.

Stewart, Katherine. "Eighty-one Percent of White Evangelicals Voted for Donald Trump. Why? The Role Abortion Played in this Election Might be Bigger than Many Think." *The Nation.* November 17, 2016. https://www.thenation.com/article/eighty-one-percent-of-white-evangelicals-voted-for-donald-trump-why/.

Stover, Johnnie M. "Nineteenth-Century African American Women's Autobiography as Social Discourse: The Example of Harriet Ann Jacobs." *College English* 66 (2003)133–54. www.ncte.org/library/NCTEFiles/store/SampleFiles/Journals/ce/CE00662nineteenth.pdf .

Tannehill, Robert C. *The Narrative Unity of Luke-Acts: A Literary Interpretation.* Vol. 2. The Acts of the Apostles. Minneapolis: Fortress, 1990.

Tenney, Merrill C. *Gospel of John.* Edited by Frank E. Gaebelein. Vol. 9. Grand Rapids, MI: Zondervan, 1981.

Thibodeau, Paul H., and Lera Boroditsky. "Metaphors We Think With: The Role of Metaphors in Reasoning." *PLoS ONE* 6 2 (2011) 1–11. http://lera.ucsd.edu/papers/crime-metaphors.pdf.

Toh, Michelle. "Sandra Bland Death. Is Waller County the Most Racist County in Texas?" *USA Update.* July 22, 2015. http://www.csmonitor.com/USA/USA-Update/2015/0722/Sandra-Bland-death-Is-Waller-County-the-most-racist-county-in-Texas-video.

Tolbert, Mary Ann. "Reading for Liberation." *Reading from this Place, Vol. 1, Social Location and Biblical Interpretation in the United States,* edited by Fernando F. Segovia and Mary Ann Tolbert, 263–76. Minneapolis: Fortress, 1995.

Townes, Emilie M. *Womanist Ethics and the Cultural Production of Evil.* New York: Palgrave Macmillan, 2006.

Trainor, Dennis Jr. "Detroit Water Crisis—a Prelude to the Privatization of Water." *DetroitWaterBrigade.org.* August 20, 2014. http://detroitwaterbrigade.org/detroit-water-crisis-prelude-privatization-water/.

Trocmé, Étienne. *Le livre des Actes et l'histoire.* Paris: Presses Universitaires de France, 1957.

Walker, Alice. "Womanist." *Search of Our Mothers' Gardens: Womanist Prose.* San Diego: Harcourt Brace, 1983.

Weil, Martin. "Death of Woman Shocked by Stun Gun in Fairfax Jail is Ruled an Accident." *Washington Post.* April 28, 2015. https://www.washingtonpost.com/local/crime/death-of-woman-shocked-by-stun-gun-in-fairfax-jail-is-ruled-an-accident/2015/04/28/7bc85f36-edfc-11e4-a55f-38924fca94f9_story.html.

Weitzer, Ronald, and Steven A. Tuch. *Race and Policing in America: Conflict and Reform.* New York: Cambridge University Press, 2006.

Weller, Sheila. "How Author Timothy Tyson Found the Woman at the Center of the Emmett Till Case." *Vanity Fair.* January 26, 2017. http://www.vanityfair.com/

news/2017/01/how-author-timothy-tyson-found-the-woman-at-the-center-of-the-emmett-till-case.

White, E. Frances. *Dark Continent of Our Bodies: Black Feminism and the Politics of Respectability*. Philadelphia: Temple University Press, 2001.

Wilder, Craig Steven. *Ebony and Ivy: Race, Slavery, and the Troubled History of America's Universities*. New York: Bloomsbury, 2014.

Williams, Demetrius K. "Acts of the Apostles." *True to Our Native Land: An African American Commentary of the New Testament*, edited by Brian K. Blount, 213–48. Minneapolis: Fortress, 2007.

Williamson, HGM, and M. Kartveit. "Samaritans." In *DJG*, 834–35.

Wilson, Brittany E. "'Neither Male nor Female': Ethiopian Eunuch in Acts 8.26–40." *New Testament Studies* 60 (2014) 403–22.

Wilson, Stephen G. *The Gentiles and the Gentile Mission in Luke-Acts*. London: Cambridge University Press, 1973.

Wimbush, Vincent L. "Introduction: Reading Darkness, Reading Scriptures." *African Americans and the Bible: Sacred Texts and Social Textures*, edited by Vincent L. Wimbush, 1–43. New York: Continuum, 2003.

Winkler, Inga T. *The Human Right to Water: Significance, Legal Status and Implications for Water Allocation*. Oxford: Hart, 2014.

Wisely, John. *Detroit Free Press*. "Detroit Not Alone in Shutting Off Water for Unpaid Bills." *USA Today*. July 27, 2014. http://www.usatoday.com/story/news/nation/2014/07/27/detroit-not-alone-in-shutting-off-water-for-unpaid-bills/13228207/.

Zack, Naomi. *White Privilege and Black Rights: The Injustice of U.S. Police Racial Profiling and Homicide*. Lanham, MD: Rowman & Littlefield, 2015.

Ziolkowski, Eric J. "The Bad Boys of Bethel: Origin and Development of a Sacrilegious Type." *History of Religions* 30 4 (1991) 331–58.

———. *Evil Children in Religion, Literature and Art, Cross-Currents in Religion and Culture*. New York: Palgrave, 2001.